Bean Bag Buddies

Bean Bag
Buddies

Nicki Wheeler

David & Charles

To Emily Honour and Alice Lulu
And for Timmy, always

A DAVID & CHARLES BOOK

First published in the UK in 2000

ISBN 0 7153 0992 7

Photography by Sean Meyers and Neil Sutherland
Book design by Casebourne Rose Design Associates
Printed in the UK by Butler and Tanner Limited
for David & Charles
Brunel House   Newton Abbot   Devon

CONTENTS

INTRODUCTION 6

TOY SAFETY 7

EQUIPMENT, MATERIALS AND
TECHNIQUES 8

CUDDLY FRIENDS 19
Teddy Bear 20 • Floppy Rabbit 23
Cute Koala 24 • Spotty Dog 25

LYING AROUND 27
Beaver 28 • Duck-billed Platypus 30
Crocodile 31 • Dragon 32

CHEEKY CREATURES 35
Little Leopard 36 • Cheeky Monkey 40
Crazy Cow 41 • Daft Duck 43

WILD THINGS 45
Peter Polar Bear 46 • Robert Rhino 48
Henry Horse 49 • Zsa-Zsa Zebra 51

FLAT FACE FRIENDS 52
Sheep Toy 53 • Sheep Pillow 54
Sheep Rug 55

ALIENS 56
Alien Bob and Friends 57

FLATTIES 58
Flat Bear 59 • Flat Pig 60
Flat Elephant 61

LITTLE 'N' LARGE 62
Frog 64 • Spider 65 • Octopus 65
Turtle 66 • Large Bean Bags 67

KNOBBLY KNEES 68
Clive Crow 69 • Funky Flamingo 71
Simon Seagull 72 • Peter Parrot 73

HAPPY HEADS 74
Smiley Faces 75 • Alien 76
Little Devil 76 • Cat 77 • Rabbit 77
Dog 78 • Lion 78 • Frog 78
Tiny Happy Heads 79

JUGGLING BABIES 81
Babies From Around the World 81

HANGING AROUND 85
Calico Doll 86 • Calico Angel 87

HAPPY HALLOWE'EN 88
Black Cat 89 • Sparkly Bat 90
Happy Ghost 91 • Pumpkin Pal 92
Hallowe'en Wreath 93

CHRISTMAS CAPERS 95
Christmas Tree 96 • Red-nosed Reindeer 97
Snowman 97 • Bright Star 98

PATTERNS 99
Stockists 127
Acknowledgements 127
Index 128

INTRODUCTION

Soft bean bag toys have taken the world by storm. These cute creatures are usually made from soft, plush-pile velour fabrics or fleece, and are filled with a mixture of polyester stuffing and plastic beans, which give them their characteristic soft, floppy appearance. Many families have at least one bean bag creature in their home, and some are possessed by the bean-bag bug and buy or collect as many as they can. Some of the toys have become highly desirable and collectable, and there is a growth in shops and internet websites devoted solely to selling and auctioning bean bag toys, some of which sell for thousands of pounds or dollars. Because bean bag toys are everywhere at the moment, I thought it was the ideal time to produce a book with instructions on how to make your own loveable bean bag characters, including projects that will be of interest to all the family. The projects include four basic patterns for traditional style bean bag toys, and four variations of toys are produced from each pattern, such as the Cuddly Friends on page 19, which feature an adorable black teddy bear, floppy bunny, cute koala and a spotty dog. Additional projects include a range of characters that will appeal to parents, teenagers, young children, babies and even pets!

All projects have complete step-by-step instructions, patterns and colour photographs. There is advice on toy safety, and a techniques section including information on which fabrics and materials to use and the basic sewing techniques required. At the back of the book, you will find the actual-size patterns needed to make all the bean bag characters. The variety of projects and techniques provides a mixture of characters which can be made by readers of all ages and abilities.

Toy Safety

All handmade toys should be safe for babies and young children to play with, and should comply with basic safety regulations. Here are some useful tips and recommendations to take into account when choosing fabrics and materials and making toys.

- All materials used, including fillings, eyes and noses, should comply with safety regulations. Most packaged items such as toy stuffing, eyes and so on, will state on the pack whether they conform to Safety Standard regulations. If you are unsure whether items meet these standards, ask the shop assistant for advice before purchasing.
- Toys shouldn't be able to catch fire easily if placed near a fire or heater, so don't choose fabrics that are highly flammable or are likely to flare up quickly if they catch fire. If you are unsure whether a fabric is suitable, ask the shop assistant for advice.
- Stuffings and fillings should be non-flammable, clean and washable, and free from any hard or sharp objects. Packets of filling and stuffing sold in large stores or craft suppliers should comply with Safety Standard regulations.
- Make sure that the toys are well constructed, with all the pieces stitched firmly together. Use safety eyes and noses which can be secured firmly in place, so that young children cannot pull or chew them off. Modern safety eyes and noses are secured in place by a metal or plastic washer on the inside of the toy (see page 16).
- You need to take extra care if you are making bean bag toys for children under three years old that any fibres, eyes and so on, cannot be pulled loose as these could cause choking if swallowed by accident. Make sure that the fur fibres cannot be pulled loose from the fur fabric, and that any eyes or noses are stitched firmly in place, rather than glued on.
- Plastic beans used for fillings should not be poured directly into the toy, but be placed in an inner lining bag. This will avoid the danger of a child choking in case the toy should split and the beans spill out. You can find more information on making lining bags in the techniques section on page 16.

EQUIPMENT, MATERIALS AND TECHNIQUES
Equipment and Materials

● ●

You don't need many tools or materials to make the projects in this book, and often you can improvise by using different materials to those suggested. However, you will find some of the following tools and instructions useful, with some handy tips on fabrics and fillings. Read the Toy Safety section on page 7 before starting any project.

NEEDLES
You'll need a good selection of needles for general hand sewing and embroidery. Long embroidery needles will be especially useful for adding cheeks and whiskers.

PINS
Use long rust-free pins, like quilting or glass-headed pins with coloured ends. When pinning fur fabrics the heads of normal pins can become lost in the fur and may be left in the fabric by mistake. This could be dangerous and lead to painful accidents for babies and young children. Glass-headed pins are easy to see and can be easily removed.

THIMBLE
A well-fitting thimble is useful when sewing, to protect your fingers and to help you push the needle through tough fabrics. Using a thimble makes sewing easier and faster once you have got used to using one.

SCISSORS
Have a selection of scissors available. Use sharp dressmaker's scissors for cutting large pieces of fabric, and sharp, pointed embroidery scissors for cutting around delicate shapes and for trimming off threads. Use a separate pair of paper scissors for cutting out paper patterns and templates – don't use your fabric scissors for cutting paper because you'll blunt them.

FABRICS

All the projects use either velour with a short or luxury pile or stretch fleece, both ideal for making bean bag creatures. Because these fabrics are increasingly used to make fashion items and accessories, they are readily available in fabric stores and good haberdashery departments, in a variety of colours and prints. Although these fabrics may seem expensive to buy by the metre or yard, you will only need a small amount to make a bean bag creature.

Fleece is a lightweight stretch polyester fabric with a fuzzy, brushed appearance on both sides, so that they look the same. It does not fray when cut and shrinks back into shape when stretched. It is easy to stitch by hand or machine and is a lovely fabric to work with.

Velour is rather like the fabric that shop-bought bean bag toys are made from, but it has a slightly longer pile. It is made from polyester with a knitted base and short, soft velvety pile and is like a cross between velvet and fur. It does not fray when cut and is easy to stitch by hand or machine.

THREADS

Use polyester rather than cotton thread for machine or hand sewing fabric pieces together, as polyester thread is strong and does not snag or break easily. It is also durable and has a slight give, making it ideal for stitching stretchy synthetic fleece and fur fabrics. For hand embroidery, use stranded embroidery cotton (floss) for eyes, mouths, noses and whiskers, or for adding toes to paws.

STUFFINGS AND FILLINGS

Plastic beans are used to give bean bag creatures their typical floppy appearance. Safety standard plastic beans are available to buy by weight from good craft outlets and mail order suppliers. There is a supplier listed in Stockists on page 127. The rest of the bean bag is filled with polyester stuffing, which is readily available from haberdashery departments or craft stores. Generally, the more expensive polyester stuffing is of better quality and gives a softer finished result.

FABRIC MARKER PENS

These are available in a wide range of colours from craft shops. They are easy to use – just draw on the fabric and when dry, iron the fabric on the wrong side to fix the dye and make it wash-proof. Always check manufacturer's instructions before use.

Techniques

• •

USING THE PATTERNS

All the patterns used in this book are clearly labelled and can be found on pages 99–126. For most projects the pattern pieces are shown as actual size, so you can just trace or photocopy them directly, but for a few others you will need to reduce or enlarge them to size, either using a photocopier or by scaling them up on graph paper as explained below. Details on sizing are provided alongside each pattern and in the project instructions. Some pattern pieces have been overlapped to fit on the page. Remember to transfer *all* the pattern markings, and label each pattern piece if tracing the pattern or resizing using the grid method. When you have finished using the paper pattern pieces, put them into a large, clearly labelled envelope to store them away safely.

ENLARGING AND REDUCING PATTERNS

The patterns are designed to be enlarged or reduced with a photocopier. Where appropriate, a degree of enlargement or reduction is suggested as a guide, but you can copy the patterns to whatever size you want. You can do this yourself or a print shop will do it for you. Alternatively, use graph paper to scale the patterns to size as explained here.

1 Trace the design onto paper and draw a box around it. Mark points at equal gaps of 1–2.5cm (½–1in) intervals along the edges, then join the points to make a grid. Number the squares along one vertical and one horizontal edge (see fig 1).

2 Draw a larger or smaller box on another piece of paper to the size you want the finished template. Draw up a grid in it with the same number of squares as the previous grid, and number them to match.

3 Copy the contents and shapes of each box accurately onto the empty grid, using the numbers along the edges as a guide (see fig 1).

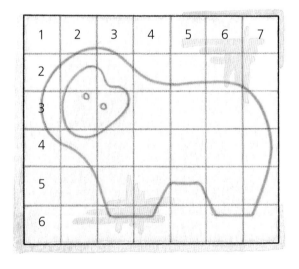
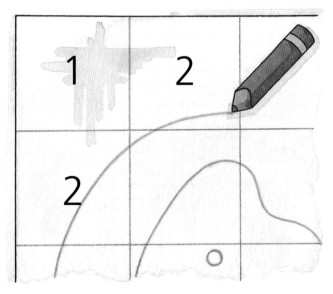

Fig 1 Using a grid to enlarge or reduce a pattern

CUTTING OUT

As some of the pattern pieces are small and complicated, rather than pinning the pieces to the fabric you may find it easier and more accurate to draw round each pattern piece on to the fabric. Place the fabric on a hard, flat surface, with the right side facing down. Place the pattern pieces onto the wrong side of the fabric, then use a pencil, chalk pencil, or a special vanishing marker pen to draw around each shape (see fig 2). Remember to transfer *all* pattern markings onto the fabric before cutting out the fabric shapes. You could also label each shape to help with identification when stitching the fabric pieces together.

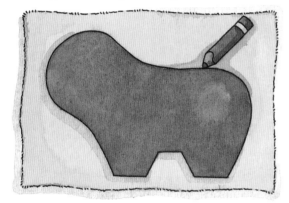

Fig 2 Drawing around a template on the wrong side of the fabric before cutting out

When you have cut out your fabric pieces and transferred all the markings, keep them together by storing them in clean, dry plastic bag. It is a good idea to keep all other project materials, such as thread and safety eyes together, as they can be easily lost.

VELOUR FABRICS

Velour fabrics may have a short pile that runs in one direction – this is called a nap. The nap usually runs in the same direction as the selvedge edges. Some of the new short-pile, velvety velour fabrics have a textured surface so that the direction of the pile can change frequently. Some fur fabrics, like fuzzy lambs' wool, does not have a nap. If you need to cut several of the same shape, cut these out *individually* rather than folding the fabric

to cut several layers. Because some of these fabrics have a pile, it can cause the fabric to slip when cutting through several layers, distorting your pattern shapes.

Some of the projects in this book use velour fabric rather than fleece. When using velour fabrics, or other fabrics with a pile, check which way the pile runs before cutting out your pattern pieces. For best results when making your bean bags, have the pile running down the body, arms, legs and head. To make sure that the pile runs in the same direction, take care when laying out your pattern pieces on to the fabric before cutting out, to ensure that the fur runs in the right direction.

FLEECE FABRICS

Fleece fabric has a fuzzy texture on both sides, and tends to be the same on both sides. If both sides are the same, you can use either side as the right side for cutting out your pattern pieces.

CUTTING OUT MORE THAN ONE SHAPE

The instructions for each project lists which pattern pieces you need to cut and how many of each. If you have to cut two of something, you should use the pattern piece to cut one shape, then reverse the pattern piece to cut the next shape (see fig 3). If you need to cut four of the same shape, you repeat this process to cut two pairs. Reversing the pattern piece, will ensure that you have the fur or nap on the right side of each shape.

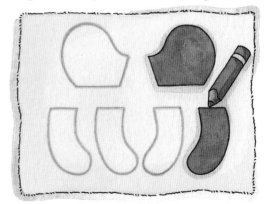

Fig 3 Lay the pattern shapes on the wrong side of the fabric and reverse the pattern when cutting out more than one shape

SEAM ALLOWANCES

All seam allowances are indicated on the patterns. For the actual-size patterns, a seam allowance of 6mm (¼in) is indicated on each pattern piece by a broken line. If you reduce the pattern to make a smaller bean bag toy, continue to use a 6mm (¼in) seam allowance, but if enlarging the pattern pieces to make much larger versions, such as the pet bean bag beds (page 67), or the sheep pillow and rug (pages 54 and 55), then use a 1.5cm (⅝in) seam allowance.

MAKING FEET AND FACES

Many of the designs use additional hand stitching and embroidery to add facial features such as mouths and whiskers, or to add toes to paws. The instructions and diagrams below show you these techniques.

STITCHES

All the stitches used in the projects are quite straightforward, but if you haven't worked some of them before or if you need a quick reminder, just follow the instructions below.

Backstitch

This stitch is used for adding mouths. Referring to fig 4, bring the needle through the fabric at 1. In one movement, insert the needle in at 2 and out at 3, so that 3 is the same distance from 1 as 1 is from 2. Repeat to work a line of stitches.

French Knots

These are small knots which are used for eyes. Bring the needle through to the front of the fabric and wind the thread twice around the needle. Hold the twisted thread firmly in place and carefully insert the needle back into the fabric to the wrong side, close to where it came out. For a larger knot, wind the thread more times round the needle (see fig 5).

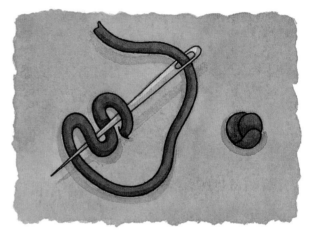

Fig 5 French knot

Running Stitch

This stitch is used for making noses and muzzles. Working from right to left, run the needle in and out of the fabric, making evenly spaced stitches of the same size (see fig 6).

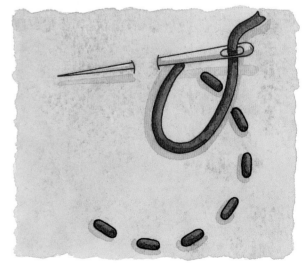

Fig 6 Running stitch

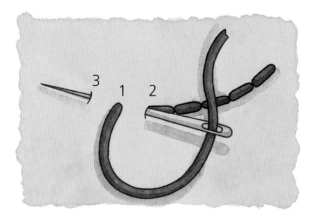

Fig 4 Backstitch

Straight Stitch

This stitch is used to add whiskers. Bring the needle through to the right side of the fabric at the starting point of a whisker and take it back through to the wrong side at the finishing point of the whisker (see fig 7). Repeat as necessary.

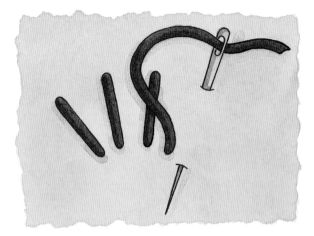

Fig 7 Straight stitch

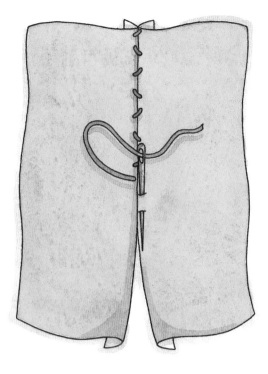

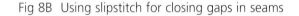
Fig 8B Using slipstitch for closing gaps in seams

Slipstitch

This useful little stitch is used to secure muzzles and noses in place (see fig 8A), and for closing gaps in fabric (see fig 8B). Working from right to left, pick up a few threads from the main fabric and then a few threads from the other piece of fabric. Repeat this, working tiny stitches quite close together.

Ladder Stitch

Ladder stitch is used to close gaps in fabric. It is stitched from the right side and is almost invisible. Turn the raw edges of the seam allowance under, then pick up small amounts of fabric on either side of the gap, pulling the thread tightly as you go, forming horizontal stitches across the gap, like the rungs of a ladder (see fig 9).

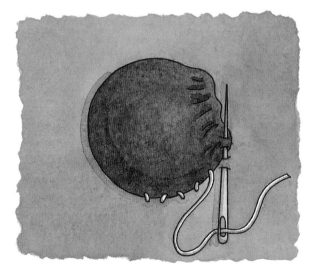

Fig 8A Using slipstitch to attach a nose to a face

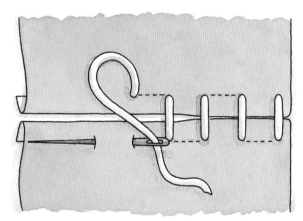

Fig 9 Ladder stitch

CHEEKS AND MUZZLES

Make a row of running stitches all around the edge of the cheek or muzzle shape. Put a ball of stuffing at the centre (see fig 10A), then pull up the ends of the threads to secure the wadding (batting) inside. Tie the ends of the threads together then trim them off (see fig 10B).

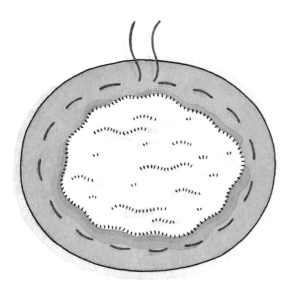

Fig 10A Make gathering stitches around the fabric and place stuffing in the centre

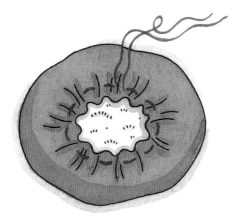

Fig 10B Pull up the gathering stitches to enclose the stuffing

Place the muzzle shape centrally over the face, pin it in place then use slipstitches to secure it. To separate the muzzle into cheeks, use a long needle to secure a length of double thread centrally at the top of the muzzle. Bring the thread about three-quarters of the way down the centre of the muzzle, insert the needle and bring it up through the fabric back to the starting point (see fig 11). Pull the thread tightly to scrunch up the fabric and divide the muzzle into cheeks. Repeat to work another stitch, then secure the thread at the starting point.

Fig 11 Long stitches used to pull the centre of the muzzle and divide it

NOSES

Make a nose in the same way as the muzzle. Make running stitches all around the edge of the cheek or muzzle shape. Put a ball of stuffing at the centre, then pull up the ends of the threads to secure the stuffing inside. Tie the ends of the threads together then trim them off. Place the nose centrally on the face and secure in place with slipstitches.

WHISKERS

When the muzzle has been stitched in place and the cheeks added, you can use long stitches to create whiskers, using two strands of stranded embroidery cotton (floss). Secure the thread to the muzzle front with a small over-stitch, then work long stitches to make three or four whiskers on each cheek (see fig 12).

Fig 12 Using long stitch to add whiskers

MOUTHS

Work the mouth with backstitch using two strands of stranded cotton (floss). You can use backstitch to add a variety of different shaped mouths to give each character a different personality (see fig 13). If you wish, you can use a chalk pencil or special vanishing marker pen to draw the mouth first.

FINGERS AND TOES

When you have finished making your creature, you may need to add fingers and toes, like the aliens on page 56. Use six strands of stranded cotton (floss) in your needle to stitch the fingers and toes as indicated on the pattern. Secure the thread at the back of the hand, foot or paw, with a small over-stitch, then push the needle right through the paw from the back to the front. Bring the needle over the curve of the finger or toe to the back of the paw, pulling tightly, and then repeat to make another stitch (see fig 14). Continue this process until you have stitched all the fingers and toes, then secure the thread at the back of the paw.

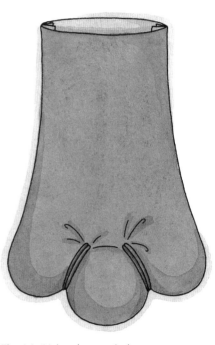

Fig 14 Using long stitches to create fingers and toes

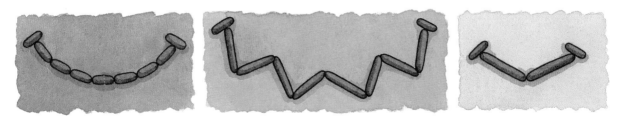

Fig 13 Using backstitch to create mouths

SAFETY EYES AND NOSES

The positions for safety eyes and noses are indicated on the pattern pieces usually by large black dots, but you can put them where you wish. Use a fabric hole punch or a sharp pair of scissors to make a small hole in the fabric where each eye or nose should be. If the fabric is liable to ladder, add a dab of craft glue around the hole to prevent this. Place the eye on the right side of the fabric, insert the long prong through the hole to the wrong side of the fabric, then push the metal or plastic washer on to the prong to secure it in place. The washers are slightly domed, so make sure that the dome faces upwards, pushing the washer down as far as it will go (see fig 15).

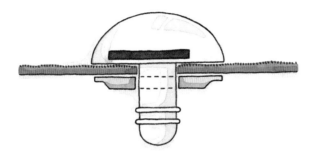

Fig 15 Adding safety eyes

ROLLED CYLINDERS

Rolled cylinders are used to make stalks and arms for the pumpkin on page 92 and the snowman on page 97. Cut the fabric to the required size, then gently roll it between your fingers to make a tight cylinder. Secure the long outer edge to the cylinder shape using small over-stitches (see fig 16).

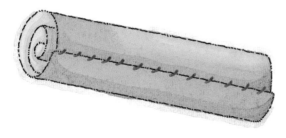

Fig 16 Making a rolled fabric tube, with the outside edge held in place with over-stitching

STUFFINGS AND FILLINGS

The bean bag toys use a mixture of polyester stuffing and small plastic beans for filling. If you are making a toy for a child under three years old, you need to put the plastic beans into an inner lining bag. This will prevent the beans from spilling out if the outer seams should be split open.

POLYESTER STUFFING

To achieve the characteristic floppy appearance of bean bag toys, you only need to lightly stuff your bean bag character. Before adding the stuffing to the toy, gently tease it out to make the stuffing puff up and make your toy softer. To add stuffing to difficult areas, use the handle of a wooden spoon or a knitting needle to push the stuffing into place.

LINING BAGS FOR PLASTIC BEANS

Some bean bag shapes such as the Happy Heads on page 75, and the Happy Hallowe'en characters on page 88, are easy to make lining bags for. Simply cut out the body shapes in lining fabric, lightly fill with a mixture of stuffing and plastic beans, then insert the bag into the body. The project instructions will tell you what to do.

For more complicated shapes, such as the Cuddly Friends on page 19, you will need to make special bags to go inside the toy, to fill the tummy and bottom area. These lining bags are made from two rectangles of lining fabric stitched together. The project instructions will tell you what size pieces to cut.

To make a lining bag, pin the lining shapes together then stitch along the two long edges and one short edge. Turn the bag right side out, then add enough plastic beans to fill the bag one third full. Pin and stitch the top edges of the lining bag together with a row of gathering stitches, then pull up the threads and secure with a knot (fig 17).

CLOSING THE GAPS

When you have added all the stuffing and plastic beans to your toy, close the remaining gap with slipstitches (see fig 8B, page 13), or with ladder stitches (see fig 9, page 13).

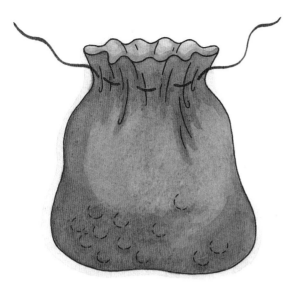

Fig 17 Securing beans in a lining bag with a line of gathering stitches along the top

ADDING A TAG

If you want your bean bag characters to be unique, then you could add a tag as a finishing touch. Fold a piece of thin card in half, draw a label shape on the card (perhaps a diamond, oval or heart shape), with part of the shape on the fold. Cut the shape from the card and open out, then design and colour in the tag in a design of your choice. Use a hole punch to cut a hole through both the thicknesses of card, thread a length of embroidery cotton through the hole and sew the cotton onto your bean bag character.

CUDDLY FRIENDS

This cute bunch of cuddly friends are based on the same pattern as a more traditional toy shape. By using this basic pattern, changing the ear and tail shapes and using different coloured fur for the body, tummy, paws and ears, you can create a lovely spotty dog, teddy bear, floppy rabbit or cute koala.

To make the cuddly friends, follow the instructions below and use the full-sized patterns on pages 102–104. Each creature is 30cm (12in) tall, which is quite large, but you could reduce this simply by reducing the pattern size on a photocopier. Each cuddly friend is made in basically the same way but with some minor alterations for each, so follow the instructions given for each character.

Teddy Bear

• •

What you will need

- Black luxury velour, 45 x 60cm (18 x 24in)
- Thin fleece for paws and ears 10 x 20cm (4 x 8in)
- Polyester lining fabric, 13 x 33cm (5 x 13in)
- Three black ball safety eyes, 11mm
- Polyester stuffing for filling
- Plastic beans
- Matching sewing thread

1 Photocopy the Cuddly Friends pattern pieces on pages 102–104, then cut out the paper shapes to use as templates. From the velour cut 2 body backs, 1 body front, 2 tails, 2 ears, 2 head backs, 2 head fronts, 1 head gusset, 2 leg fronts and 2 upper arms. From the thin fleece cut 2 paws and 2 ears. From the lining fabric cut 2 rectangles 12 x 16cm (4¾ x 6¼in). Refer to Cutting Out on page 11 if necessary.

2 To make the head, place the head backs together with right sides facing, then pin and stitch together between the black dots. With right sides facing, pin and stitch the head fronts together from the nose to the neck, between the two black dots.

3 To add the head gusset, pin the gusset shape to the head front with right sides facing, matching the black dot at the front of the gusset to the black dot at the nose of the head front, then match the white dots on the gusset to the white dots at the top of each head front piece. Pin and stitch the gusset in place.

4 To make the ears, pin and stitch one velour and one fleece ear shape together with right sides facing, leaving the bottom edge open. Repeat for the other ear then turn right side out.

5 Place each ear with the fleece side down, over each head gusset seam on the head front, so that they face inwards and all the raw edges meet (see fig 18). Pin and tack (baste) the ears in place.

6 With right sides facing, pin and stitch the head front and back together, matching the white dots at the bottom, and the black dots at the top of the head. Turn the head right side out, so that the ears are on the outside. Add the two eyes at the place indicated on the head gusset template, then add the nose at the place where the gusset and front head seams all meet (see Safety Eyes and Noses page 16).

7 To make the tummy, fold the body front shape in half with right sides facing. Stitch the darts at the top and bottom, then snip the darts to make them lie flat (see fig 19).

Sewing a dart in place

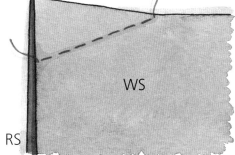

Cutting the dart to lie flat

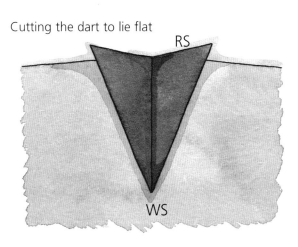

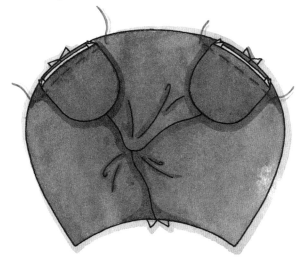

Fig 18 Adding ears

Fig 19 Making darts

8 With right sides facing, pin and stitch the fleece paws to the velour upper arm shapes. With right sides facing, pin the arms to each side of the tummy, matching the black dots, then stitch in place. Repeat for the leg fronts, but match the white dots on the legs with the white dots on the lower edges of the tummy shape.

9 To make the tail, pin and stitch the velour tail shapes together with right sides facing, leaving the bottom edge open, then turn the tail right side out.

10 To make the body back, place the body back shapes together with right sides facing, matching the black and white dots at the back, then pin the back seams together between the black and white dots. Stitch the lower back seam together between the black dots, and stitch the back seam together between the white dots and the line marked on the pattern, to leave a gap.

11 Open out the back body shape and press the seams flat. With right sides facing, pin the tail to the lower edge of the bottom dart (see fig 20). With right sides facing, fold the back body shape in half, bringing the two edges of the bottom dart together, so that the tail is sand-wiched between the two layers. Pin and stitch the edges of the dart together to secure the tail in place.

12 With right sides facing, pin the front and back body pieces together, matching all the dots carefully. Pin and stitch the two layers together around the shoulders, arms, legs and tummy, leaving the top neck edge open.

13 To add the head to the body, insert the head inside the body so that the neck

edges meet and right sides are facing. Match the head side seams to the body shoulder seams, the front seam to the tummy dart seam, and the back head seam to the body back seam. Pin and stitch the head in place, around the neck edge. Turn the bear right side out, through the gap at the back of the body.

14 To make the lining bag, pin the lining rectangles together then stitch along the two long edges and one short edge. Turn the bag right side out, then add enough plastic beans to fill the bag one third full. Pin and stitch the top edges of the lining bag together with a row of gathering stitches, then pull up the threads and secure with a knot (see Lining Bags page 16). Lightly fill the head, legs and arms with polyester stuffing, then insert the lining bag into the body and secure the back seam with ladder stitching (see page 13).

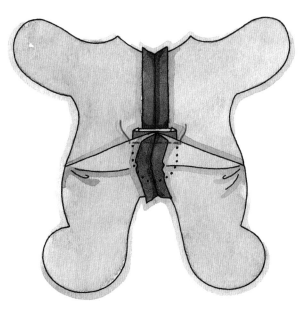

Fig 20 Adding the tail

Floppy Rabbit

What you will need

- Luxury beige velour, 45 x 60cm (18 x 24in)
- Thin fleece for paws and ears, 20cm (8in) square
- Polyester lining fabric, 13 x 33cm (5 x 13in)
- Two black ball safety eyes, 11mm
- Small pom-pom for nose
- Polyester stuffing for filling
- Plastic beans
- Matching sewing thread

1 Photocopy the Cuddly Friends pattern pieces on pages 102–104, then cut out the paper shapes to use as templates. From the velour cut 2 body backs, 1 body front, 2 tails, 2 ears, 2 head backs, 2 head fronts, 1 head gusset, 2 leg fronts and 2 upper arms. From the thin fleece cut 2 paws and 2 ears. From the lining fabric cut 2 rectangles 12 x 16cm (4¾ x 6¼in).

2 Follow steps 2–4 of the Teddy Bear instructions on page 21.

3 Fold the bottom edge of each ear in half at the fold line, with the fleece side inside. Place the ears on the head gusset at either side of the gusset seam, with the fleece side down, and the folded edges facing towards the head centre. Make sure that the ears face inwards and all the raw edges meet (see fig 18, page 21). Pin and tack (baste) the ears in place.

4 Follow step 6 of the Teddy Bear instructions on page 21, but stitch a small pom-pom in place for the nose.

5 Follow steps 7–14 of the Teddy Bear instructions. Finally, pinch each ear at the outer edge to make the ears bend forward, then secure the bend in place with a few hand stitches.

Cute Koala

What you will need

- Luxury grey velour, 50cm (20in) square
- White fleece for tummy, paws and ears, 25cm (10in) square
- Polyester lining fabric, 13 x 33cm (5 x 13in)
- Two black ball safety eyes, 11mm
- Safety koala nose, 21mm
- Polyester stuffing for filling
- Plastic beans
- Matching sewing thread

1 Photocopy the Cuddly Friends pattern pieces on pages 102–104, then cut out the paper shapes to use as templates. From the velour cut 2 body backs, 2 tails, 2 ears, 2 head backs, 2 head fronts, 1 head gusset, 2 front legs and 2 upper arms. From the white fleece cut 1 body front, 2 paws and 2 ears. From the lining fabric cut 2 rectangles 12 x 16cm (4¾ x 6¼in).

2 Follow steps 2–4 of the Teddy Bear instructions on page 21.

3 Make a small tuck at the bottom edge of each ear, as indicated on the pattern by the dotted lines. Place each ear with the fleece side down, at either side of the head gusset seam on the head front, so that they face inwards and all the raw edges meet (see fig 18, page 21). Pin and tack (baste) the ears in place.

4 To finish, follow steps 6–14 of the Teddy Bear instructions on pages 21 and 22.

Spotty Dog

. . . .

What you will need

- Luxury spotty velour, 50cm (20in) square
- Fleece for tummy, paws and ears, 20 x 30cm (10 x 12in)
- Polyester lining fabric, 13 x 33cm (5 x 13in)
- Two black ball eyes, 11mm
- Safety dog nose, 20mm
- Polyester stuffing for filling
- Plastic beans
- Matching sewing thread

1 Photocopy the Cuddly Friends pattern pieces on pages 102–104, then cut out the paper shapes to use as templates. From the spotty velour cut 2 body backs, 2 tails, 2 ears, 2 head backs, 2 head fronts, 2 front legs and 2 arms. From the fleece cut 1 head gusset, 1 body front and 2 ears. From the lining fabric cut 2 rectangles 12 x 16cm (4¾ x 6¼in).

2 Follow steps 2–4 of the Teddy Bear instructions on page 21.

3 Fold the bottom edge of each ear towards the centre, with the fleece side inside the folds. Place each ear with the fleece side down, over each head gusset seam on the head front, so that they face inwards and all raw edges meet (see fig 18, page 21). Pin and tack (baste) the ears in place.

4 Follow steps 6 and 7 of the Teddy Bear instructions on page 21. Then, follow step 8, but do not add paws to the upper arms as the Spotty Dog does not have paws.

5 With right sides facing, pin and stitch the fur tail shapes together, leaving the bottom edge open. Turn the tail right side out, then squash the bottom edges together, so that the seams lie on top of each other. This should make the tail tip curl up slightly.

6 Follow steps 10–14 of the Teddy Bear instructions on page 22 to finish.

LYING AROUND

This project concentrates on a traditional bean bag shape to make creatures that crawl or lie on their tummy, with legs sprawled out at the side. Choose from a brown beaver with a flat black tail, a delightful duck-billed platypus with large flat bill and tail, a cute crocodile with bumps down its back, or a floppy dragon with big ears and wings. The same basic pattern is used to make all four creatures, but with some modifications to each. The beaver and platypus have short round faces and separate tails, whilst the dragon and crocodile are more complicated, with longer faces, joined tails and additional wings or spikes. From nose to tail, the beaver measures 28cm (11in), the platypus is 33cm (13in) and the dragon and crocodile each measure 35cm (14in) long.

Beaver

● ●

What you will need

- Brown velour, 40cm (16in) square
- Black luxury velour, 10 x 20cm (4 x 10in)
- Polyester lining fabric, 15 x 25cm (6 x 10in)
- Two black ball safety eyes, 11mm
- One small black pom-pom
- Polyester stuffing for filling
- Plastic beans
- Matching sewing thread

1 Photocopy the Lying Around pattern pieces on pages 105–109, then cut out the paper shapes to use as templates. For the beaver, cut the upper body and body base shapes with the *short* legs. From the brown velour cut 1 body base, 2 upper bodies, 2 legs, 4 ears, 1 neck, 1 face and 1 head base. From the black velour cut 2 tails. From the lining cut 2 rectangles 12 x 15cm (4¾ x 6in). Refer to Cutting Out on page 11 if necessary.

2 With right sides facing, pin and stitch the ears together in pairs, leaving the bottom edge open, then turn the ears right side out.

3 Place each ear right side down, over the right side of the face between the white dots, so that they face inwards and all the raw edges meet (see fig 21). Pin and tack (baste) the ears in place.

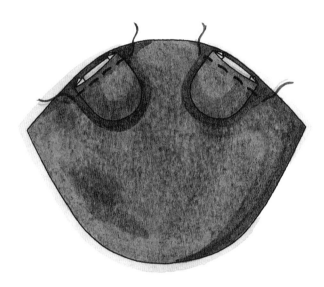

Fig 21 Adding the ears

4 With right sides facing, pin and stitch the face and neck shapes together, matching the black dots, to form the upper head. Add the two eyes at the place indicated on the pattern (see Safety Eyes and Noses page 16). With right sides facing, pin and stitch the upper head and head base shapes together, matching the black dots on the base with the upper head side seams, and leaving the top edge open. Turn the head right side out.

5 With right sides facing, pin and stitch the tail shapes together, leaving the top edge open. Turn the tail right side out, then add a small amount of polyester stuffing.

6 Place the tail right side down, over the right side of the body base between the black dots, so that it faces inwards and all the raw edges meet. Pin and tack (baste) the tail in place.

7 With right sides facing, pin and stitch the upper body shapes together along the centre back, leaving a gap as indicated on the pattern. Then, with right sides facing, pin and stitch the upper body and body base shapes together, leaving the neck edge open.

8 To add the head to the body, insert the head inside the body so that the neck edges meet and right sides are facing. Match the head side seams to the body side seams, and the body centre back seam with the notch on the neck edge. Pin and stitch the head and body around the neck edge. Clip into the seams on the neck and body where necessary, then turn right side out through the gap at the centre back seam.

9 To make the lining bag, pin the lining rectangles together then stitch along the two long edges and one short edge. Turn the bag right side out, then add enough plastic beans to fill the bag one third full. Pin and stitch the top edges of the lining bag together with a row of gathering stitches, then pull up the threads and secure with a knot (see fig 17, page 17). Lightly fill the head and legs of the body with polyester stuffing, then insert the lining bag into the body and secure the back seam with ladder stitching (see page 13).

10 To finish the beaver, make a nose by stitching a pom-pom in place at the front of the face.

Duck-Billed Platypus

· ·

What you will need

- Blue luxury velour, 30 x 40cm (12 x 16in)
- Blue fleece, 30cm (12in) square
- Polyester lining fabric, 15 x 25cm (6 x 10in)
- Two black ball safety eyes, 11mm
- Polyester stuffing for filling
- Plastic beans
- Matching sewing thread

1 Photocopy the Lying Around pattern pieces on pages 105–109, then cut out the paper shapes to use as templates. For the platypus, cut the upper body and body base shapes with no legs. From the velour cut 1 body base, 2 upper bodies, 1 neck, 1 face and 1 head base. From the fleece cut 2 bills, 2 tails, 4 front feet and 4 back feet. From the lining fabric cut 2 rectangles 12 x 15cm (4¾ x 6in).

2 With right sides facing, pin and stitch the bill shapes together, leaving the bottom edge open. Turn the bill right side out, then add a small amount of polyester stuffing. Repeat this process for the tail and the front and back feet, matching the feet together in pairs.

3 Place the bill over the right side of the face, between the black dots, so that it faces inwards and all the raw edges meet. Pin and tack (baste) the bill in place.

4 To make the head, follow step 4 of the Beaver instructions on page 29.

5 To add the tail follow step 6 of the Beaver instructions. Then add the front and back feet in the same way, but matching the white dots.

6 To finish the Platypus, follow steps 7–9 of the Beaver instructions, but you will only need to add the polyester stuffing to the head.

Crocodile

What you will need
- Green luxury velour, 40 x 50cm (16 x 20in)
- Polyester lining fabric, 15 x 25cm (6 x 10in)
- Two black ball safety eyes, 11mm
- Polyester stuffing for filling
- Plastic beans
- Matching sewing thread

1 Photocopy the Lying Around pattern pieces on pages 105–109, then cut out the paper shapes to use as templates. For the crocodile, cut the upper body and body base shapes with *long* legs. From the velour cut 1 body base, 2 upper bodies, 2 legs, 2 tails, 2 spikes, 1 neck, 1 face and 1 head base. From the lining fabric cut 2 rectangles 12 x 15cm (4¾ x 6in).

2 With right sides facing, pin the spikes together and stitch from the white dots around the spikes, leaving the bottom straight edge open. Clip into the seam at each spike, then turn the spikes right side out. If necessary, use a pin to carefully tease out each spike, then tack (baste) the bottom straight edges together.

3 Place the back spikes right side down over the right side of one upper body shape, between the white dots so that the spikes face inwards and all the raw edges meet. Pin, tack (baste) and stitch the spikes in place.

4 With right sides facing, pin and stitch the upper body shapes together along the centre back, leaving a gap as indicated on the pattern.

5 With right sides facing, pin one tail shape to the body base, and one to the upper body, matching the black dots. Stitch the tail shapes in place, then press the seams open. Then, with right sides facing, pin the upper body and body base shapes together, then stitch around the legs and tail leaving the neck edge open.

6 To make the head, follow step 4 of the Beaver instructions on page 29. To finish the crocodile, follow steps 8 and 9 of the Beaver instructions.

Dragon

· ·

What you will need
• Cranberry luxury velour, 50cm (20in) square
• Polyester lining fabric, 15 x 25cm (6 x 10in)
• Two black ball safety eyes, 11mm
• Polyester stuffing for filling
• Plastic beans
• Matching sewing thread

1 Photocopy the Lying Around pattern pieces on pages 105–109, then cut out the paper shapes to use as templates. For the dragon, cut the upper body and body base shapes with *long* legs. From the velour cut 1 body base, 2 upper bodies, 2 legs, 2 tails, 4 wings, 4 ears, 1 neck, 1 face and 1 head base. From the lining fabric cut 2 rectangles 12 x 15cm (4¾ x 6in).

2 To make the ears and head, follow steps 2–4 for the Beaver on pages 28 and 29, but at the end of step 3 fold the ears in half along the bottom edge, and tack (baste) the fold in place. For step 4, place the ears folded side down, with the fold facing towards the centre of the head (see fig 22).

necessary, turn the wings right side out, then machine stitch through the centre of each wing as indicated by the dotted lines on the pattern. Fold the wings in half along the bottom edge and tack (baste) the fold in place.

4 Place the wings with the folded side down, over the right side of each upper body shape, matching the black dots so that the wings face inwards and all the raw edges meet. Pin and tack (baste) the wings in place (see fig 23).

5 To complete the body and tail of the dragon, follow steps 4 and 5 of the Crocodile instructions on page 31.

6 To make the head, follow step 4 of the Beaver instructions on page 29, then to finish the dragon, follow steps 8 and 9 of the Beaver instructions.

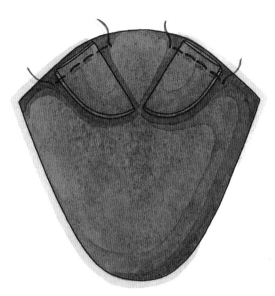

Fig 22 Adding the dragon's ears

3 With right sides facing, pin and stitch the wings together in pairs, leaving the bottom straight edge open. Clip into the seams where

Fig 23 Adding the dragon's wings

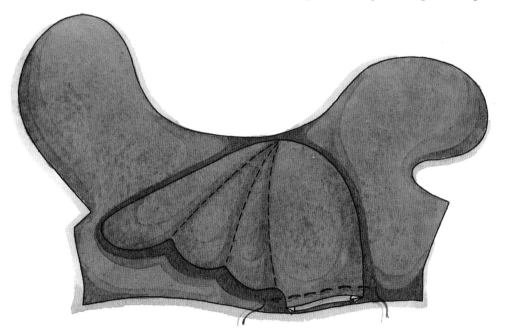

CHEEKY CREATURES

This group of cheeky creatures are all made from the same basic pattern, using a mixture of fleece and fun print luxury velour fabrics. The cheeky monkey, little leopard and crazy cow all measure 25cm (10in) from head to toe, while the daft duck is 18cm (7in) tall. The individual characters are created by adding ears, tails, noses, horns, beaks and wings to the basic body shape. You could use this shape to make anything from a dog, sheep or alien to a little person made in pink fleece – just let your imagination run away with you.

Little Leopard

• •

What you will need

- Leopard-print velour, 50cm (20in) square
- Contrast fleece, 20cm (8in) square
- Polyester lining fabric, 30cm (12in) square
- Two brown safety eyes, 12mm
- One small pom-pom
- Polyester stuffing for filling
- Plastic beans
- Matching sewing thread
- Contrast embroidery thread

1 Photocopy the Cheeky Creatures pattern pieces on pages 110–112, then cut out the paper shapes to use as templates. From the leopard-print velour cut 1 body front, 2 body backs, 1 body base, 2 head backs, 1 upper face, 2 lower faces, 2 upper arms, 2 lower arms, 2 upper legs, 2 lower legs, 2 tails and 2 ears. From the fleece cut 2 ears, 2 paws, 2 foot paws and 1 muzzle. From the lining fabric cut 1 body front, 2 body backs, 1 body base, 2 head backs, 1 upper face and 2 lower face shapes. Refer to Cutting Out on page 11 if necessary.

2 To make the face, place the velour head backs together with right sides facing, then pin and stitch together between the black dots. With right sides facing, pin and stitch the lower face shapes together from the nose to the neck, between the two black dots. Then, with right sides facing, pin and stitch the lower face and upper face shapes together, matching the white and black dots.

3 To make the ears, with right sides facing, pin and stitch one velour and one fleece ear shape together, leaving the bottom edge open. Repeat for the other pair, then turn the ears right side out.

4 Place each ear with the fleece side down, over the right side of the upper face, between the squares marked on the pattern pieces, so that they face inwards and all the raw edges meet (see fig 24). Pin and tack (baste) the ears in place.

5 To make the head, with right sides facing, pin and stitch the head front and back together, matching the white dots at the bottom and side seam, and the black dots and seam notch at the top of the head. Turn the head right side out so that the ears are on the outside. Add the two eyes at the place indicated on the pattern by the large black dots (see Safety Eyes and Noses page 16).

Fig 24 Adding the leopard's ears

6 To make the tummy, fold the body front shape in half with right sides facing, stitch the darts at the top and bottom, then snip the darts to make them lie flat (see fig 19 page 21).

7 With right sides facing, pin and stitch the paws to the upper arm shapes. With right sides facing, pin and stitch one upper arm and one lower arm together, leaving the top edge open for turning. Repeat for the other pair, then turn the arms right side out. Repeat the process for the legs, but matching the foot paws to the lower legs.

8 Add a small amount of polyester stuffing to all the paws, then use embroidery thread to stitch the toes as indicated on the pattern (see Fingers and Toes page 15). Make a tuck at the top edge of each arm as indicated on the pattern, then pin and tack (baste) the tuck in place (see fig 25).

9 Place each arm with paw side down, over the right side of the body front, matching the black dots on the arms and the body sides, then pin and tack (baste) the arms in place. Repeat for the legs, but place them paw side up, matching the white dots on the legs with the white dots on the lower edges of the body front (see fig 26).

10 To make the tail, with right sides facing, pin and stitch the tail shapes together, leaving the bottom edge open, then turn the tail right side out. Squash the top edges of the tail together so that the seams lie over each other and then pin together.

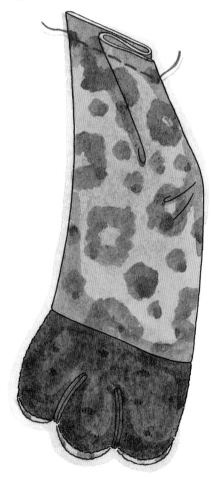

Fig 25 Making the tuck at the top of the arm

Fig 26 Adding arms and legs to the body

11 To make the back, with right sides facing, place the body back shapes together, then pin the back seam between the white dots. Stitch the back seam between the white dots and the lines marked on the pattern, to leave a gap. Then, with right sides facing, pin and tack (baste) the tail to the base of the body back, laying the tail centrally over the back seam (see fig 27).

Fig 27 Adding the tail

12 With right sides facing, pin and stitch the body front and body back pieces together, matching all the dots and making sure that the arms are sandwiched between the two layers. Then, with right sides facing, pin and stitch the body base to the lower edge of the body, matching the notch at the body base front with the tummy dart, and matching the black and white dots, making sure that the legs and tail are tucked inside.

13 To add the head to the body, insert the head inside the body so that the neck edges meet and right sides are facing. Match the head side seams to the body side seams, the front seam to the tummy dart seam, and the back head seam to the body back seam. Pin and stitch the head around the neck edge, then turn the creature right side out through the gap at the body back.

14 The lining bag is the same shape as the head and body so make it up from the lining fabric pieces in the same way as the outer body, but do not add the ears, arms, legs or tail (see Lining Bags page 16). Lightly fill the head of the lining bag with polyester stuffing, then fill the bottom of the body with plastic beans and top up with polyester stuffing. Close the gap at the back of the bag with ladder stitches (see page 13) to keep the beans and stuffing secure. Insert the lining bag into the outer body, then secure the back seam with ladder stitches.

15 Make gathering stitches around the muzzle shape, place some stuffing at the centre, pull up the gathering threads and secure them with a knot. Place the muzzle onto the face, just below the eyes, and stitch in place. Use two strands of contrast embroidery thread to add the mouth and whiskers (see page 15). Finally, stitch the small pom-pom for the nose at the top of the muzzle.

Cheeky Monkey

● ●

What you will need

- Tan fleece, 50cm (20in) square
- Contrast fleece, 20cm (8in) square
- Polyester lining fabric, 30cm (12in) square
- Two amber safety eyes, 14mm
- One small pom-pom
- Polyester stuffing for filling
- Plastic beans
- Matching sewing thread
- Contrast embroidery thread

1 Photocopy the Cheeky Creatures pattern pieces on pages 110–112, then cut out the paper shapes to use as templates. From the tan fleece cut 1 body front, 2 body backs, 1 body base, 2 head backs, 1 upper face, 2 lower faces, 2 upper arms, 2 lower arms, 2 upper legs, 2 lower legs, 2 tails and 2 ears. From the contrast fleece cut 2 ears, 2 paws, 2 foot paws, 2 tail tips and 1 muzzle. From the lining fabric cut 1 body front, 2 body backs, 1 body base, 2 head backs, 1 upper face and 2 lower face shapes.

2 Follow steps 2 and 3 of the Little Leopard instructions on page 37, matching the fleece ears together in pairs. Follow steps 4–9 of the Little Leopard instructions.

3 For the tail, pin and stitch the tail and the tail tip shapes together, with right sides facing, then still with right sides facing, pin and stitch the tail shapes together, leaving the bottom edge open. Turn the tail right side out and add a small amount of polyester stuffing to the tail tip. Squash the top edges of the tail together so that the seams lie over each other and then pin them together.

4 Follow steps 11–15 of the Little Leopard instructions on page 39 but on step 15 you do not need to add whiskers.

Crazy Cow

• •

What you will need
- Spotty velour, 35cm (14in) square
- Black fleece, 25cm (10in) square
- Scraps of white and pink fleece
- Polyester lining fabric, 30cm (12in) square
- Two black ball eyes, 11mm
- Polyester stuffing for filling
- Plastic beans
- Matching sewing thread
- Black embroidery thread

1 Photocopy the Cheeky Creatures pattern pieces on pages 110–112, then cut out the paper shapes to use as templates. From the spotty velour cut 1 body front, 2 body backs, 1 body base, 4 upper arms, 2 upper legs and 2 lower legs. From the black fleece cut 2 head backs, 2 lower faces, 2 ears, 4 cow hoofs, 2 upper hoofs, 2 lower hoofs and 1 tail. From the white fleece cut 1 upper face, 1 muzzle and 4 horns. From the pink fleece cut 2 ears. From the lining fabric cut 1 body front, 2 body backs, 1 body base, 2 head backs, 1 upper face and 2 lower face pieces.

2 Follow steps 2 and 3 of the Little Leopard instructions on page 37, but for step 3 match a pink and a black ear shape together in pairs. Then, fold the ears in half along the bottom edge so that the pink fleece is on the inside and tack (baste) the fold in place. Stitch the horns together in pairs, turn right sides out and add a small amount of polyester stuffing.

3 Place the horns over the right side of the upper face, between the squares marked on the pattern piece, then place each ear with the pink fleece side down, between the squares and triangles so that they face inwards and all the raw edges meet (see fig 28). Pin and tack (baste) the ears and horns in place.

4 Follow steps 5 and 6 of the Little Leopard instructions on pages 37 and 38. Then, with right sides facing, pin and stitch the paws to the upper arm shapes. With right sides facing, pin and stitch two upper arms together in pairs, leaving the top edge open. Repeat for the other pair, then turn the arms right side out. Repeat the process for the legs, but match the upper legs with the upper hoofs and the lower legs with the lower hoofs.

5 Follow step 8 of the Little Leopard instructions but do not add the toes. Place each arm over the right side of the body front, matching the black dots on the arms and the body sides, then pin and tack (baste) the arms in place. Repeat for the legs matching the white dots on the legs with the white dots on the lower edges of the body front (see fig 26 page 38).

6 Cut the fringe at the base of the tail as indicated by the lines on the pattern, then roll the tail into a cylinder shape and secure the long edge with slipstitches (see Rolled Cylinders page 16).

7 Follow steps 11–15 of the Little Leopard instructions on page 39 but for step 15 add two French knots for the nostrils instead of adding a mouth and whiskers, and do not add the pom-pom nose.

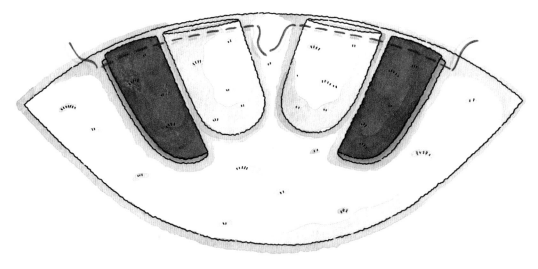

Fig 28 Adding the cow's ears and horns

Daft Duck

• •

What you will need
• White fleece, 40cm (16in) square
• Yellow fleece, 15cm (6in) square
• Polyester lining fabric, 30cm (12in) square
• Two blue safety eyes, 10mm
• Polyester stuffing for filling
• Plastic beans
• Matching sewing thread

1 Photocopy the Cheeky Creatures pattern pieces on pages 110–112, then cut out the paper shapes to use as templates. From the white fleece cut 1 body front, 2 body backs, 1 body base, 2 head backs, 1 upper face, 2 lower faces, 4 wings and 2 tails. From the yellow fleece cut 2 beaks and 4 feet. From the lining fabric cut 1 body front, 2 body backs, 1 body base, 2 head backs, 1 upper face and 2 lower faces.

2 With right sides facing, pin and stitch the beak shapes together, and then the feet shapes together in pairs. Leave the top edges open, then turn the shapes right side out. Add a small amount of polyester stuffing to the beak, then, with right sides facing, pin and tack (baste) the beak to the upper face, matching the notch on the beak to the black dot on the upper face, so the beak faces inwards and all the raw edges meet.

3 Follow steps 2, 5 and 6 for the Little Leopard instructions on pages 37 and 38.

4 With right sides facing, pin and stitch the wings together in pairs, leaving the top edge open, then turn the wings right sides out. Make a tuck at the top edge of each wing as indicated on the pattern, then pin and tack (baste) the tuck in place (see fig 25 page 38).

5 Place each wing over the right side of the body front, matching the black dots on the wings and the body sides, then pin and tack (baste) the wings in place. Repeat for the feet, matching the white dots on the feet with the white dots on the lower edges of the body front (see fig 26 page 38).

6 Stitch the darts in the tail shapes (see fig 19 page 21). With right sides facing, pin and stitch the tail shapes together, leaving the bottom edge open, then turn the tail right side out.

7 Follow steps 11–14 for the Little Leopard instructions on page 39 to finish.

WILD THINGS

This group of standing bean bag characters are all creatures found in the wild. They are all made from the same pattern and stand 12cm (4¾in) from head to toe, and are 18cm (7in) long from nose to tail. A mixture of fleece and plain and patterned velour are used to make the creatures, and thick acrylic wool is used to make the mane and tail for the dappled horse and stripy zebra. Use the pattern to make a polar bear, rhino, zebra or horse Alternatively you could leave the horn off the rhino to turn it into a hippo; make the bear in brown velour or fleece to turn it into a grizzly bear; or make a white horse and add a horn to transform it into a unicorn.

Peter Polar Bear

What you will need

- White fleece, 30 x 50cm (12 x 20in)
- Polyester lining fabric, 13 x 33cm (5 x 13in)
- Two blue safety eyes, 10mm
- Polyester stuffing for filling
- Plastic beans
- Matching sewing thread

1 Photocopy the Wild Things pattern pieces on pages 100–101, then cut out the paper shapes to use as templates. From the white fleece cut 2 side bodies, 2 under bodies, 1 head gusset, 4 feet and 6 ears. From the lining fabric cut 2 rectangles 12 x 16cm (4¾ x 6¼ in). Refer to Cutting Out on page 11 if necessary.

2 Use the six ear pieces to make three ears, one of which will act as a tail. With right sides facing, pin and stitch the ear shapes together in pairs, leaving the bottom straight edge open. Turn the shapes right side out.

3 Take each body side and carefully cut the dart at the top of the head, as indicated on the pattern by the solid black line. With right sides facing and raw edges matching, pin and tack (baste) each ear at the base of each dart. Then, with right sides facing, fold the head in half, bringing the two edges of the dart together so that the ears are sandwiched between the two layers. Pin and stitch the edges of the dart together to secure the ears in place.

4 With right sides facing, pin and tack (baste) the tail onto one body side shape. Place the tail between the white dots so that it faces inwards and all the raw edges meet.

5 To make the upper body, with right sides facing, pin and stitch the body sides together, between the black dots at the head and bottom.

6 To make the body base, with right sides facing, pin the under body shapes together between the black dots. Stitch from each black dot to the lines indicated on the pattern, leaving a gap for turning. Then, with right sides facing, pin and stitch the body base and head gusset shapes together along the neck edge, matching the white and black dots.

7 To make the body, open out the upper body and body base shapes, then place them together with right sides facing. Pin and stitch the shapes together between the black dots at the base of each back leg and at the creature's bottom. At the body front, pin and stitch the body base and head gusset to the upper body, carefully matching the white dots at the base of each front leg, the white dots at the neck seam and body side, the notches around the nose and head, and the black dot at the top of the head.

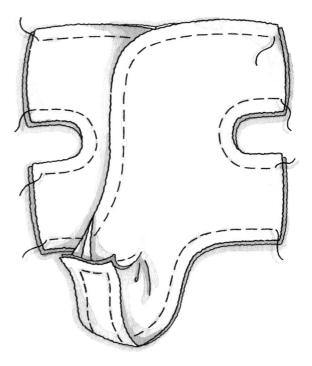

Fig 29 Adding the body to the base and gusset

Pin and stitch around the inner leg, then clip into the seams where necessary (see fig 29).

8 With right sides facing, pin and stitch the feet to the base of each leg, matching the notches on the foot with the side seams on each leg. Turn the creature right side out, through the gap in its tummy. Finally, add the two eyes at the place indicated by the large black dots on the head gusset template (see Safety Eyes and Noses page 16).

9 To make the lining bag, pin and stitch the lining rectangles together along the two long edges and one short edge. Turn the bag right side out, then add enough plastic beans to fill the bag one third full. Pin and stitch the top edges of the lining bag together with a row of gathering stitches, then pull up the threads and secure with a knot (see Lining Bags, page 16). Lightly fill the head and legs with polyester stuffing, insert the lining bag into the body and secure the back seam with ladder stitches (see page 13).

Robert Rhino

What you will need

- Grey luxury velour, 30 x 50cm (12 x 20in)
- Polyester lining fabric, 13 x 33cm (5 x 13in)
- Two black ball safety eyes, 11mm
- Polyester stuffing for filling
- Plastic beans
- Matching sewing thread

1 Photocopy the Wild Things pattern pieces on pages 100–101, then cut out the paper shapes to use as templates. From the velour cut 2 side bodies, 2 under bodies, 1 head gusset, 2 tails, 2 horns, 4 feet and 4 ears. From the lining fabric cut 2 rectangles each 12 x 16cm (4¾ x 6¼in).

2 With right sides facing, pin and stitch the ear shapes together in pairs, leaving the bottom straight edge open, then turn the shapes right side out. Repeat this process with the horn and tail shapes.

3 To complete Robert Rhino, follow steps 3–9 of the Peter Polar Bear instructions on page 47. Add a small amount of stuffing to the horn. To finish, turn under a small hem at the bottom edge of the horn, place the horn in the correct position on the head and slipstitch in place.

Henry Horse

• •

What you will need

- Dapple-patterned velour, 30 x 50cm (12 x 20in)
- Polyester lining fabric, 13 x 33cm (5 x 13in)
- Two black ball safety eyes, 11mm
- Thick black wool
- Scrap of thin ribbon or tape
- Polyester stuffing for filling
- Plastic beans
- Matching sewing thread

1 Photocopy the Wild Things pattern pieces on pages 100–101, then cut out the paper shapes to use as templates. From the velour cut 2 side bodies, 2 under bodies, 1 head gusset, 4 feet and 4 ears. From the lining fabric cut 2 rectangles 12 x 16cm (4¾ x 6¼in).

2 With right sides facing, pin and stitch the ear shapes together in pairs, leaving the bottom straight edge open, then turn the shapes right side out.

3 To add the ears to the body, follow step 3 of the Peter Polar Bear instructions on page 47.

4 To make the mane, lay the wool over a length of ribbon or tape, allowing for 2.5cm (1in) loops at each side. Stitch the wool to the ribbon or tape by hand or machine (see fig 30), making a 6cm (2¼in) length of looped wool for the mane and a 1cm (½in) length for the fringe.

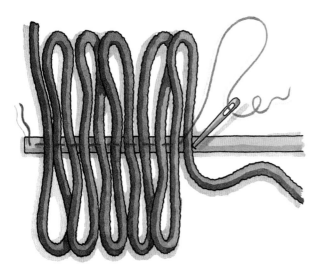

Fig 30 Making the mane

5 To add the mane to the body, lay one side body shape right side up. Fold the tape in half along the length, so that the wool loops are all facing in the same direction. Lay the tape along the top edge of the side body, starting at the back black dot and working down so that the wool loops are facing inwards, then tack (baste) the tape in place (see fig 31). To add the fringe, repeat the process, but add the short length of looped wool to the top edge of the head gusset.

6 To make the tail, cut eight 10cm (4in) lengths of thick black wool and bunch them up. Lay the bunch of wool over the right side of the side body with the mane attached, and tack (baste) in place between the white dots, so that the tail faces inwards.

7 To complete making Henry Horse, follow steps 5–9 of the Peter Polar Bear instructions on page 47. Finish the tail by tying the lengths of wool into a knot at the base. Trim the tail, mane and fringe to the desired length to finish.

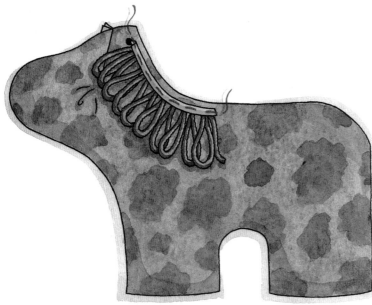

Fig 31 Adding the mane
to the side body

Zsa-Zsa Zebra

What you will need

- Stripy velour, 30 x 50cm (12 x 20in)
- Polyester lining fabric, 13 x 33cm (5 x 13in)
- Two black ball safety eyes, 11mm
- Thick black wool
- Scrap of thin ribbon or tape
- Polyester stuffing for filling
- Plastic beans
- Matching sewing thread

1 Photocopy the Wild Things pattern pieces on pages 100–101, then cut out the paper shapes to use as templates. From the velour cut 2 side bodies, 2 under bodies, 1 head gusset, 4 feet and 4 ears. From the lining fabric cut 2 rectangles 12 x 16cm (4¾ x 6¼ in).

2 To make the ears, follow step 2 of the Henry Horse instructions on page 49. To add the ears to the body, follow step 3 of the Peter Polar Bear instructions on page 47.

3 To make the mane and tail, follow steps 4–6 of the Henry Horse instructions.

4 To complete Zsa-Zsa Zebra, follow steps 5–9 of the Peter Polar Bear instructions on page 47. Finally, finish the tail by tying the lengths of wool into a knot at the tail base. Finish by trimming the tail, mane and fringe to the desired length.

FLAT FACE FRIENDS

Instead of counting sheep, these lovely flat face sheep will help children to go to sleep! A simple two-piece pattern is used to make a small bean bag toy from soft fleece fabric – an ideal comforter for children to cuddle in bed. The pattern is enlarged to make a soft fleece sheep-shaped pillow and a huge rug made from fun fur fabric and fleece. The small sheep toy is filled with plastic beans to give it the characteristic bean-bag feel, whilst the sheep pillow is like a large cushion filled with soft polyester stuffing. The flat faces on the pillow and rug are filled with beans to give the faces more character, and all the sheep have boggle eyes which are either plastic safety eyes or hand-made from felt.

Sheep Toy

What you will need
• White fleece or fun fur, 35cm (14in) square
• Black fleece, 18cm (7in) square
• Polyester lining fabric, 35cm (14in) square
• Two safety boggle eyes, 12mm
• Polyester stuffing for filling
• Plastic beans

1 Photocopy the Flat Face Friends pattern pieces on page 113, then cut out the paper shapes to use as templates. From the white fleece or fun fur cut 2 tails and 2 bodies. From the black fleece cut 4 feet, 2 ears and 1 face. From the lining fabric cut 2 rectangles 9 x 18cm (3½ x 7in). Refer to Cutting Out page 11 if necessary.

2 To make the sheep front, pin the face to one body shape as indicated on the pattern. Fold each ear along the dotted line, slip the straight edges of the ears under the face shape so that the black dots match, and then pin in place. Tack (baste) around the face shape securing the ears in place, then stitch the face in place close to the outer edge. Finally, add the two safety eyes to the face in the positions indicated on the pattern (see Safety Eyes and Noses page 16).

3 To make the tail, place the two tail shapes together, right sides facing, then pin, tack (baste) and stitch around the curved edge, leaving the bottom edge open. Turn the tail right side out then insert a small amount of stuffing.

4 Place the tail over the body front so that it faces inwards, matching the black dots so that all the raw edges meet. Pin and tack (baste) the tail in place. Do the same for the feet, adding them to the body front and back. Stitch the feet in place, then press the seams open.

5 Fold the ear shapes out of the way over the face and pin them securely in place. Then, with right sides facing, place the front and back body shapes together and pin and tack (baste) the layers together. Stitch around the body shape, leaving a 9cm (3½in) gap along the top edge, then turn right side out.

6 Pin, tack (baste) and stitch the lining shapes together along one short and both long sides. Turn the bag right side out, half fill with plastic beans and secure the gap with slipstitches. Lightly fill the sheep legs, head and bottom with polyester stuffing, insert the lining bag and secure the gap with slipstitches.

Sheep Pillow

• •

What you will need

- White fleece, 0.7m x 150cm (¾ yd x 60in) wide
- Black fleece, 0.3m x 150cm (⅜ yd x 60in) wide
- Pink fleece, 30cm (12in) square
- Calico, 0.7m x 150cm (¾ yd x 60in) wide
- Two safety boggle eyes, 25mm
- Polyester stuffing for filling
- Plastic beans
- Matching sewing thread

1 Enlarge the Flat Face Friends pattern pieces on page 113 using the grid method on page 10. Enlarge the pillow to a total width of 75.5cm (29½in), by a total height of 59cm (23¼in) – or choose your own size. Cut out the paper shapes to use as templates. From the white fleece cut 2 tails and 2 bodies. From the black fleece cut 4 feet, 2 ears and 1 face. From the pink fleece cut 2 ears. From the calico cut 2 faces. For the pillow lining, lay the sheep body template on the calico and draw round it with a pencil, then use the foot template to draw a foot at the base of each leg. Cut 2 of these shapes from calico.

2 To make the ears, with right sides facing, pin and stitch one pink and one black ear shape together, leaving the bottom edge open. Repeat for the other pair then turn the ears right side out. Fold the ears along the dotted line with the pink fleece on the inside of the fold, then pin and tack (baste) the fold in place along the bottom edges of each ear.

3 To make the face lining bag, pin, tack (baste) and stitch the two calico face shapes together taking a 2cm (¾in) seam allowance and leaving a gap for turning. Turn right side out, half fill with a mixture of polyester stuffing and plastic beans, then secure the gap with slipstitches.

4 Place the face lining bag on the body front, as indicated on the pattern, then pin and tack (baste) in place. Add the two safety eyes to the black fleece face shape in the positions indicated on the pattern (see Safety Eyes and Noses page 16), then lay the face shape over the lining bag and pin in place. Slip the straight edges of each ear under the face so that the black dots match and then pin in place. Tack (baste) around the face shape securing the ears in place, then stitch the face in place close to the outer edge.

5 Follow steps 3–5 on page 53 for the Flat Face Sheep Toy, but leave a 30cm (12in) gap for turning.

6 Pin and stitch the calico body lining shapes together, leaving a 30cm (12in) gap along one edge. Turn the lining bag right side out, fill generously with polyester stuffing, then secure the gap with slipstitches. Insert the lining bag into the sheep pillow shape and secure the gap with slipstitches.

Sheep Rug

• •

What you will need
- White sheep fun fur, 1.6m x 150cm (1¾ yd x 60in) wide
- Black fleece, 0.5m x 150cm (⅝ yd x 60in) wide
- White fleece, 20cm (8in) square
- Polyester stuffing for filling
- Polyester wadding (batting)
- Plastic beans
- Matching sewing thread

1 Enlarge the Flat Face Friends pattern pieces on page 113 using the grid method on page 10. Enlarge the rug to a total width of 101cm (40in), by a total height of 70.5cm (29½in) – or choose your own size. Cut out the paper shapes to use as templates. From the white fun fur cut 2 tails, 2 ears and 2 body shapes. From the black fleece cut 4 feet, 2 ears and 1 face. From the calico cut 2 faces. For the eyes, draw a 10cm (4in) diameter circle in paper for the eye and a 2.5cm (1in) diameter circle for the pupils. Using the paper circles as templates, cut 2 large circles in white fleece and 2 small circles in black fleece.

2 Follow steps 2 and 3 for the Flat Face Sheep Pillow, but for step 2, match one fur and one black fleece ear together in pairs, and fold the ear so that the black fleece is on the inside of the fold.

3 For the face, follow step 4 for the Flat Face Sheep Pillow but do not add the eyes. For the eyes, make gathering stitches around the edge of each white fleece circle, place some polyester stuffing at the circle centre, pull up the gathering threads and secure with a knot. Stitch a black circle to the front of each eye, then stitch the eyes to the face (see Safety Eyes and Noses page 16).

4 Follow steps 3 and 4 on page 53 for the Flat Face Sheep Toy. With right sides facing upwards, lay each body shape over the wadding (batting). Pin and tack (baste) the shapes to the wadding (batting), then cut away the excess wadding (batting) by cutting around each body shape.

5 Follow step 5 on page 53 for the Flat Face Sheep Toy but leave a 30cm (12in) gap for turning. Turn the rug through to the right side and secure the gap with slipstitches

ALIENS

These fun aliens are all based on the same principle of stitching two shapes together to make a flat bean bag, with the addition of legs and antennae. Being so simple to make, these alien flatties would make ideal projects for children and beginners. The alien measures 24cm (9½in) from antennae to toe.

Alien Bob and Friends

• •

What you will need for each alien
• Fleece or silver Lycra, 30cm (12in) square
• Polyester lining fabric, 30cm (12in) square
• Two boggle eyes, 12mm
• One small pom-pom
• Polyester stuffing for filling
• Plastic beans
• Matching sewing thread

1 Photocopy the Alien Flattie pattern pieces on page 116, then cut out the paper shapes to use as templates. From the fleece or Lycra cut 2 bodies, 2 small legs, 2 big legs, 2 antennae and 1 nose. From the lining fabric cut 2 bodies. Refer to Cutting Out on page 11 if necessary.

2 With right sides facing, fold each antenna in half along the length and pin and stitch it along the long edge and one short edge. Turn each antenna right side out and tie a knot at the stitched end.

3 To make the legs, start with right sides facing, and pin and stitch the leg shapes together in pairs, leaving the top edge open. Turn the legs right side out and add a small amount of polyester stuffing to each foot.

4 Add the safety eyes on one body shape in the positions indicated on the pattern (see Safety Eyes and Noses page 16). Hand stitch a pom-pom in place for the tummy button, as indicated on the pattern.

5 Place the legs over the right side of the body front so that they face inwards, matching the black dots so that all the raw edges meet, then pin, tack (baste) and stitch them in place. Do the same with both the antenna, matching the white dots.

6 With right sides facing, pin, tack (baste) and stitch the two body shapes together, making sure that the legs are inside. Leave a 7.5cm (3in) gap at the base, then turn the body right side out. Repeat this process to make the lining bag. Lightly fill the bag with polyester stuffing and plastic beans, then secure the gap with slipstitches. Insert the bag into the body, then secure the gap with ladder stitching (see page 13).

7 Make gathering stitches around the nose shape, place some stuffing at the centre, pull up the gathering threads and secure them with a knot. Place the nose onto the face directly under the eyes, and stitch in place (see Noses page 14).

FLATTIES

These cute creatures are all based on the same principle as the aliens on page 56, that of stitching two shapes together to make a flat bean bag. The bear, elephant and pig are all made from the same pattern, with the addition of ears, tails and an elephant's trunk. Because these Flatties are so easy to make, they would be ideal projects for children and beginners. The bear and pig measure 21cm (8¼in) from bottom to snout, and the elephant is 28cm (11in) long from bottom to trunk.

Flat Bear

• •

What you will need
- Luxury velour, 30 x 40cm (12 x 16in)
- Polyester lining fabric, 15 x 25cm (6 x 10in)
- Two brown safety eyes, 12mm
- Two small pom-poms
- Polyester stuffing for filling
- Plastic beans
- Matching sewing thread

1 Photocopy the Flatties pattern pieces on pages 114–115, then cut out the paper shapes to use as templates. From the velour cut 1 body base, 1 upper body, 1 head and 4 ears. From the lining fabric cut 2 rectangles each 12 x 15cm (4¾ x 6in).

2 To make the ears, start with right sides facing and pin the ears together in pairs. Stitch around the curved edge, leaving the bottom edge open, then turn the ears right side out. Make gathering stitches along the bottom edge of each ear, pull up the threads and secure with a knot.

3 Place the ears over the right side of the body front so that they face inwards, matching the black dots so that all the raw edges meet, then pin and tack (baste) and stitch them in place.

4 With right sides facing, pin and stitch the head to the upper body, matching the notches. Add the safety eyes as indicated on the pattern (see Safety Eyes and Noses page 16).

5 With right sides facing, pin, tack (baste) and stitch the two velour body shapes together, leaving a 7.5cm (3in) gap at the base, then turn the body right side out.

6 To make the lining bag, pin the lining rectangles together then stitch along the two long edges and one short edge. Turn the bag right side out and add enough plastic beans to fill the bag one third full. Pin and stitch the top edges of the lining bag together with a row of gathering stitches, then pull up the threads and secure with a knot (see fig 17, page 17). Lightly fill the head and legs of the body with polyester stuffing, then insert the lining bag into the body and secure the back seam with ladder stitching (see page 13).

7 To finish your flat bear, stitch a pom-pom on the face for a nose, and one at the base for a tail.

Flat Pig

. . . .

What you will need
• Luxury velour, 30 x 40cm (12 x 16in)
• Polyester lining fabric, 15 x 25cm (6 x 10in)
• Two black ball safety eyes, 11mm
• Thin elastic, 7cm (2¾ in) long
• Polyester stuffing for filling
• Plastic beans
• Matching sewing thread
• Black stranded cotton (floss)

1 Photocopy the Flatties pattern pieces on pages 114–115, then cut out the paper shapes to use as templates. From the velour cut 1 body base, 1 upper body, 1 head, 1 tail, 1 snout and 4 ears. From the lining fabric cut 2 rectangles each 12 x 15cm (4¾ x 6in).

2 Follow step 2 of the Flat Bear instructions. With right sides facing, fold the tail in half along the length, then pin and stitch along the long edge and curved edge. Stitch the ends of the elastic to each end of the tail, then turn the tail right side out.

3 Place the tail over the right side of the upper body so that it faces inwards, matching the white dots so that all the raw edges meet, then pin and stitch it in place.

4 Follow steps 3–6 of the Flat Bear instructions on page 59.

5 For the nose, make gathering stitches around the nose shape, place some stuffing at the centre, pull up the gathering threads and secure them with a knot. Stitch the nose to the front of the head, then use stranded cotton (floss) to work two French knots for the nostrils (see page 12).

Flat Elephant

What you will need
- Luxury velour, 40cm (16in) square
- Polyester lining fabric, 15 x 25cm (6 x 10in)
- Two black ball safety eyes, 11mm
- Thin elastic, 7.5cm (3in) long
- Polyester stuffing for filling
- Plastic beans
- Matching sewing thread

1 Photocopy the Flatties pattern pieces on pages 114–115, then cut out the paper shapes to use as templates. From the velour cut 2 body base shapes, 2 trunks, 4 ears and 1 tail. From the lining fabric cut 2 rectangles each 12 x 15cm (4¾ x 6in).

2 Follow step 2 for the Flat Bear instructions on page 59.

3 With right sides facing, fold the tail in half lengthways, then pin and stitch along the long edge and curved end. Turn right side out, and tie a knot at the stitched end. Now follow step 3 for the Flat Pig.

4 Place the ears over the right side of the body base so that they face inwards, matching the black dots so that all the raw edges meet, then pin and tack (baste) and stitch them in place.

5 With right sides facing, pin and stitch each trunk to each body base, matching the white dots. Take one body shape and stitch one end of the elastic to the trunk tip, and the other end to the seam, where the trunk and head are joined. Add the safety eyes as indicated on the pattern (see Safety Eyes and Noses page 16).

6 To finish the elephant, follow steps 5 and 6 of the Flat Bear instructions on page 59, making sure that the ears are tucked well inside when stitching the two shapes together.

LITTLE 'N' LARGE

These simple bean bags are all made from the same basic shape and can be made as small toys or as oversized bean bags, which are filled with polystyrene balls and are ideal for kids' bedrooms or as comfy pet beds. The toys are 23cm (9in) diameter, while the large bean bags measure 84cm (33in) in diameter, with removable outer covers so they can be easily washed. On page 64 you will find listed the basic materials needed to make any of the small bean bag toys, with extra materials listed separately under each character. The basic instructions are the same but with minor alterations, so follow the instructions listed for the individual characters and also refer to the instructions for the frog bean bag toy on page 64.

LITTLE TOYS

• • • • • • • • • • • • • • • • • • • •

What you will need for each toy
• Polyester lining fabric, 35cm (14in) square
• Polyester stuffing for filling
• Plastic beans
• Matching sewing thread
• Embroidery thread for mouth

Frog

• • • • • • • • • • • • • • • • • • • •

Additional materials
• Green fleece, 30 x 50cm (12 x 20in)
• Two safety boggle eyes, 18mm

1 Photocopy the Little 'n' Large pattern pieces on page 117, then cut out the paper shapes to use as templates. From the green fleece cut 1 body base, 1 upper body, 4 body sides and 8 frog legs. From the lining fabric cut 1 body base, 1 upper body and 4 body sides. Refer to Cutting Out on page 11 if necessary.

2 With right sides facing, pin and stitch the fleece body sides together along the short side edges. When you have joined all four sides, you will have a fabric loop with a narrow top edge and a wide bottom edge. Repeat this process for the lining.

3 To make the body shape, start with right sides facing, pin and stitch the upper body to the narrow edge of the fabric loop, matching the body side seams with the notches on the upper body. Repeat this process for the lining. Add the two safety eyes to the body as indicated on the pattern (see Safety Eyes and Noses page 16).

4 Pin the legs together in pairs with right sides facing. Stitch around the curved edges

leaving the bottom edge open, then turn the legs right side out.

5 Place the legs over the right side of the body base so that they face inwards, matching the black dots so that all the raw edges meet. Pin, tack (baste) and stitch them in place.

6 With right sides facing, pin and stitch the body to the base, matching the side seams with the notches on the base, making sure that the legs are inside. Leave a 10cm (4in) gap, then turn the body right side out. Repeat this process to make the lining bag. Lightly fill the bag with polyester stuffing and plastic beans, then secure the gap with slipstitches. Insert the bag into the body and secure the gap with slipstitches.

7 To finish the frog, work a wobbly mouth with backstitches using six strands of stranded cotton (floss) (see Mouths page 15).

The Spider and Octopus are made in basically the same way but with slightly different legs. They both have eight legs but the Spider has knotted feet and the Octopus has elasticised legs. Follow the basic instructions below, and then the leg instructions for either the Spider or Octopus.

Spider

Additional materials

- Red fleece, 30 x 40cm (12 x 16in)
- Red fine fleece, 45cm (18in) square
- Two black safety eyes, 11mm

Octopus

Additional materials

- Blue fleece, 30 x 40cm (12 x 16in)
- Blue fine fleece, 45cm (18in) square
- Two blue safety eyes, 20mm
- Narrow elastic, 72cm (28in) long

1 Photocopy the Little 'n' Large pattern pieces on page 117, then cut out the paper shapes to use as templates. From the fleece cut 1 body base, 1 upper body and 4 body sides. From the fine fleece cut 16 spider/octopus legs. From the lining cut 1 body base, 1 upper body and 4 body sides.

2 Follow steps 2 and 3 of the Frog instructions on page 64.

3 To make the legs for the Spider and the Octopus, begin by pinning the legs together in pairs, right sides facing, then stitch around the curved edges leaving the bottom edge open.
   For the Spider legs: turn the legs right side out, then tie a knot at the stitched end of each leg for feet.
   For the Octopus legs: cut the elastic into eight 9cm (3½in) lengths. Stitch a length at the curved end of each leg, then turn right side out and secure the loose end of elastic at the open edge of each leg.

4 Arrange the legs around the outer edge of the body base, evenly spaced, and with all raw edges meeting, then pin, tack (baste) and stitch them in place. To finish, follow steps 6 and 7 of the Frog instructions on page 64.

Turtle

• •

Additional materials

• Light green fleece, 35cm (14in) square
• Dark green fleece, 15cm (6in) square
• Yellow fleece, 20 x 30cm (8 x 12in)
• Two amber safety eyes, 10mm

1 Photocopy the Little 'n' Large pattern pieces on page 117, then cut out the paper shapes to use as templates. From the light green fleece cut 1 body base, 1 upper body and 2 body sides. From the dark green fleece cut 2 body sides. From the yellow fleece cut 2 heads, 2 tails and 8 turtle legs. From the lining fabric cut 1 body base, 1 upper body and 4 body sides.

2 Follow step 2 of the Frog instructions on page 64, matching alternate dark green and light green body side shapes. Then follow step 3 for the Frog instructions, leaving out the eyes.

3 Follow step 4 for the Frog instructions to make the head, tail and legs of the turtle. Add the eyes to the head as indicated on the turtle head pattern (see Safety Eyes and Noses page 16), then fill the head with a small amount of polyester stuffing.

4 Place the head and tail over the body base so that they face inwards, matching the white dots, so that all the raw edges meet. Pin, tack (baste) and stitch in place. Repeat for the legs, matching the black dots.

5 Follow step 6 of the Frog instructions, then make a mouth by using six strands of stranded cotton (floss) to work a long stitch along the seam line of the head (see Mouths page 15).

LARGE BEAN BAGS

• •

These are larger versions of the little toys and are made in exactly the same way. Listed below are the basic materials needed for each large bean bag, followed by the extra materials needed for each individual character.

What you will need for each large bean bag
- Calico, 1m x 115cm (1⅛ yd x 45in) wide
- Polystyrene balls, 1 cubic ft
- Polyester stuffing for filling
- Two safety eyes, 30mm
- Matching sewing thread
- Matching zip 40cm (16in) long

Additional materials
Frog
- Green fleece 1.3m x 150cm (1⅜ yd x 60in) wide

Spider
- Red fleece 1.5m x 150cm (1⅝ yd x 60in) wide

Octopus
- Blue fleece 1.5m x 150cm (1⅝ yd x 60in) wide

Turtle
- Lilac fleece 0.8m x 150cm (⅞ yd x 60in) wide
- Blue fleece 0.5m x 150cm (⅝ yd x 60in) wide
- Purple fleece 0.3m x 150cm (⅜ yd x 60in) wide

1 To make an oversized bean bag, enlarge the Little 'n' Large pattern pieces on page 117 using the grid method described on page 10. The body base circular pattern piece needs to be 58cm (23in) in diameter, with all the other pattern pieces enlarged accordingly. Cut out the paper shapes to use as templates.

2 To make up your large bean bag character, follow the instructions for the same bean bag toy character but add a zip to the body base. To do this, cut a 38cm (15in) slit at the centre of the body base. Place the zip centrally under the slit, then pin, tack (baste) and stitch the zip in place. Because fleece doesn't fray, the edges don't need to be neatened or turned under.

3 The lining bag is made from calico as it is much tougher. Fill the calico bag with polystyrene balls rather than plastic beans and polyester stuffing.

KNOBBLY KNEES

These colourful birds make great bean bag creatures, and with their big beaks, fat bodies, long legs, knobbly knees and funny feet, they are sure to make you smile. They sit 15cm (6in) tall and are 23cm (9in) long from beak to tail. You can use the pattern to make any bird you like – as the head and tummy are made from separate pattern pieces, you can vary the colours you use. The crow and flamingo are one colour all over, with coloured beaks and legs, whilst the parrot and seagull have different colours for the head, tummy, wings and tail. By altering the colour of the body and the length of the legs, you could make any bird you like – use long legs for a flamingo, stork or ostrich, and short legs for a duck or puffin.

Clive Crow

• •

What you will need

- Black fleece, 40 x 50cm (16 x 20in)
- Yellow fleece, 30cm (12in) square
- Polyester lining fabric, 13 x 33cm (5 x 13in)
- Two amber safety eyes, 10mm
- Polyester stuffing for filling
- Plastic beans
- Matching sewing thread

1 Photocopy the Knobbly Knees pattern pieces on pages 118–119, then cut out the paper shapes to use as templates. From the black fleece cut 2 side bodies, 1 under body gusset, 2 heads, 2 tails and 4 wings. From the yellow fleece cut 1 upper beak, 1 lower beak, 4 feet and 2 strips for the legs 5 x 23cm (2 x 9in). From the lining fabric cut 2 rectangles 12 x 16cm (4¾ x 6¼ in). Refer to Cutting Out on page 11 if necessary.

2 To make the wings, start with right sides facing, and pin and stitch the wing shapes together in pairs, leaving the top edge open. Turn the wings right side out.

3 Place each wing over the right side of each side body, matching the notches so all the raw edges meet. Pin and tack (baste) the wings in place.

4 To make the upper body, with right sides facing place a head shape over a side body shape, sandwiching the wing between them and matching the black and white dots. Pin and stitch the head and side body together, securing the wing in place. Repeat for the other head and side body shapes.

5 With right sides facing, place the body shapes together then pin and stitch from the top of the head, along the back to the base, between the white dots, leaving a gap as indicated on the pattern.

6 To make the legs, fold each long strip in half along the length so that the edges meet. Pin and stitch each strip along the length, to make a tube, then turn each tube right side out. Tie a knot at the centre of each tube for the knees.

7 Take two foot shapes and cut a small cross on them as indicated on the pattern, to form a small hole – this shape will form the top of the foot. With right sides facing, place the foot shapes together in pairs, matching a foot with a cross with one without a cross. Pin and stitch all around the edge of the feet, then turn each foot right side out, through the small hole (see fig 32).

8 To attach the feet to the legs, turn under a small hem at one end of each leg, place this turned edge over the hole on the top of the foot, with the leg seam at the back of the foot, then hand stitch the leg to the foot (see fig 33).

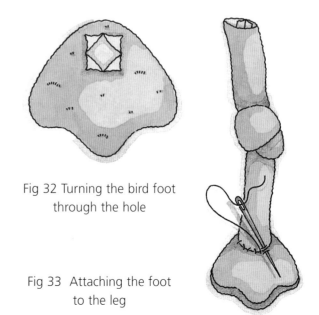

Fig 32 Turning the bird foot through the hole

Fig 33 Attaching the foot to the leg

pattern, then pin and tack (baste) the folds in place. Insert the tail through the gap at the body base, matching the notches so that all the raw edges meet, with the folded edges facing towards the gusset. Pin and stitch the tail in place through all the layers.

12 To make the beak, with right sides facing, fold the lower beak shape in half and stitch the dart in place. Then, with right sides facing, pin the upper and lower beak shapes together matching the white dots and notches, then stitch around the curved edge between the white dots and notches.

13 Turn the beak right side out, then insert the beak inside the head so that the raw edges meet and right sides are facing. Match the seams on the lower beak with the body side seams, and the white dot on the upper beak with the white dot at the head seam. Pin, tack (baste) and stitch the beak in place, then turn the bird right side out through the gap at the body back. The beak, wings, tail and legs should now be on the outside of the body. Add the eyes as indicated on the pattern (see Safety Eyes and Noses page 16).

9 With right sides facing, place each leg over the right side of the body, between the black dot and the dotted line. Match the leg seam to the dotted line, so that the legs face inwards and all the raw edges meet. Pin and tack (baste) the legs in place.

10 With right sides facing, pin the under body gusset to the upper body, matching the white and black dots from the top to the base of the gusset and upper body. Make sure that the legs and wings are enclosed inside the body shape, then stitch the gusset in place.

11 To make the tail, pin and stitch the tail shapes together, with right sides facing, leaving the top edge open. Turn the tail right side out. Fold the tail sides towards the centre notch, as indicated by the dotted lines on the

14 To make the lining bag, pin the lining shapes together then stitch along the two long edges and one short edge. Turn the bag right side out, then add enough plastic beans to fill the bag one third full. Pin and stitch the top edges of the lining bag together with a row of gathering stitches, then pull up the threads and secure with a knot (see Lining Bags page 16). Lightly fill the bird head with polyester stuffing, then insert the lining bag into the body and secure the back seam with ladder stitching (see page 13).

Funky Flamingo

What you will need

- Pink fleece, 40 x 50cm (16 x 20in)
- Dark pink fleece, 30 x 35cm (12 x 14in)
- Polyester lining fabric, 13 x 33cm (5 x 13in)
- Two pink safety eyes, 10mm
- Polyester stuffing for filling
- Plastic beans
- Matching sewing thread

1 Photocopy the Knobbly Knees pattern pieces on pages 118–119, then cut out the paper shapes to use as templates. From the pink fleece cut 2 side bodies, 1 under body gusset, 2 heads, 2 tails and 4 wings. From the dark pink fleece cut 1 upper beak, 1 lower beak, 4 feet and 2 strips for the legs 5 x 33cm (2 x 13in). From the lining fabric cut 2 rectangles 12 x 16cm (4¾ x 6¼in).

2 To make your Funky Flamingo, follow steps 2–14 for Clive Crow instructions. The flamingo is made in exactly the same way as the crow, but the flamingo has much longer legs.

Simon Seagull

● ●

What you will need

- Grey fleece, 30cm (12in) square
- White fleece, 30 x 40cm (12 x 16in)
- Beige fleece, 30cm (12in) square
- Polyester lining fabric, 13 x 33cm (5 x 13in)
- Two blue safety eyes, 10mm
- Polyester stuffing for filling
- Plastic beans
- Matching sewing thread

1 Photocopy the Knobbly Knees pattern pieces on pages 118–119, then cut out the paper shapes to use as templates. From the grey fleece cut 2 side bodies, 2 wings and 1 tail. From the white fleece cut 1 under body gusset, 2 heads, 1 tail and 2 wings. From the beige fleece cut 1 upper beak, 1 lower beak, 4 feet and 2 strips for the legs 5 x 23cm (2 x 9in). From the lining fabric cut 2 rectangles 12 x 16cm (4¾ x 6¼in).

2 To make the wings, pin one grey and one white wing shape together, with right sides facing, then repeat for the other pair. Stitch the wings together around the curved edge, leaving the top edge open, then turn the wings right side out.

3 Place each wing, white side down, over the right side of the side body shapes, matching the notches, so that all the raw edges meet. Pin and tack (baste) the wings in place.

4 Follow steps 4–10 of the Clive Crow instructions on pages 69 and 70.

5 With right sides facing, pin and stitch the grey and white tail shapes together, leaving the top edge open, then turn the tail right side out. Fold the tail sides towards the centre notch as indicated on the pattern, so the grey is on top and the white fleece is inside the fold. Pin and tack (baste) the folds in place. Insert the tail through the gap at the body base, matching the notches so that all the raw edges meet and the folded edges face towards the gusset. Pin and stitch the tail in place through all the fabric layers.

6 To complete Simon Seagull, follow steps 12–14 of the Clive Crow instructions on page 70.

Peter Parrot

● ●

What you will need
• Red fleece, 20 x 25cm (8 x 10in)
• Blue fleece, 30cm (12in) square
• Green fleece, 20cm (8in) square
• Yellow fleece, 30cm (12in) square
• Polyester lining fabric, 13 x 33cm (5 x 13in)
• Two black ball safety eyes, 11mm
• Polyester stuffing for filling
• Plastic beans
• Matching sewing thread

1 Photocopy the Knobbly Knees pattern pieces on pages 118–119, then cut out the paper shapes to use as templates. From the blue fleece cut 2 side bodies, 2 wings and 1 tail. From the red fleece cut 1 under body gusset and 2 heads. From the green fleece cut 1 tail and 2 wings. From the yellow fleece cut 1 upper beak, 1 lower beak, 4 feet and 2 strips for the legs 5 x 23cm (2 x 9in). From the lining fabric cut 2 rectangles 12 x 16cm (4¾ x 6¼in).

2 Follow steps 2 and 3 of the Simon Seagull instructions on page 72, but in step 2 match a blue and green wing together, and in step 3 place the blue side face down.

3 Follow steps 4–10 of the Clive Crow instructions on pages 69 and 70.

4 For the tail, follow step 5 of the Simon Seagull instructions, but stitch the blue and green tail shapes together, then fold the tail so that the green fleece is on top, and the blue fleece is underneath the fold.

5 To complete Peter Parrot, follow steps 12–14 of the Clive Crow instructions on page 70.

HAPPY HEADS

This bunch of cute bean bag faces are all made from the same pattern and are really easy to make. Choose from a cheeky little devil, an alien, a cat, a rabbit, a dog, a lion, a frog and a little boy and girl – or use the basic pattern to make any creature you like. The large happy heads are about 12.5cm (5in) diameter, and you could sit them on your desk or computer in the office, or on a shelf at home. They make ideal juggling balls, or just throw them around to relieve stress! The tiny bean bag faces are 6.5cm (2⅛in) diameter, and are made by reducing the pattern to create miniature alien 'zipper friends' for children to hook onto bags and jackets, to make into smiley face badges and hair scrunchies. For adults, there is even a bunch of little devil fridge magnets.

Basic Happy Head

● ●

The basic materials needed to make a head shape are listed here. Each head, however, has its own character so any extra materials needed are listed separately under each character. The instructions for each character are basically the same with minor alterations for the facial expressions and ears. Follow the instructions listed for that character, and also refer to the instructions for the Smiley Faces below.

What you will need for each head

- Fleece (any colour), 30cm (12in) square
- Polyester lining fabric, 15 x 30cm (6 x 12in)
- Polyester stuffing for filling
- Plastic beans
- Matching sewing thread
- Embroidery thread for mouth
- Fabric glue

Smiley Faces

● ●

Additional materials

- Two safety boggle eyes, 18mm
- Thick wool for hair
- Scrap of ribbon or fleece for hair bow
- Darning needle

1 Photocopy the Happy Heads pattern pieces on pages 120–121, then cut out the paper shapes to use as templates. For each head, cut from the fleece 4 ears, 2 heads, 1 base, 1 cheek and 1 nose. From the lining fabric cut 1 base and 2 heads. Refer to Cutting Out on page 11 if necessary.

2 To make the ears, start with right sides facing and pin and stitch two ear shapes together, leaving the bottom edge open. Repeat for the other pair then turn the ears right side out.

3 Place the ears over one head shape to make the head front and so that the ears face inwards, matching the white dots so all raw edges meet. Pin and tack (baste) the ears in place. Add the two safety boggle eyes to the head front in the place indicated on the pattern by the white dots (see Safety Eyes and Noses page 16).

4 With right sides facing, pin and stitch the head shapes together around the curved edge. With right sides facing, pin the base to the bottom straight edges of the head shape, matching the side seams with the notches on the base. Stitch around the base, leaving a 7.5cm (3in) gap at the back, then turn the head right side out. Repeat this process to make the lining bag. Lightly fill the bag with polyester stuffing and plastic beans, then secure the gap with slip-stitches. Insert the bag into the head, then secure the gap at the base with slipstitches.

5 The two cheeks are formed from one piece of fabric rather like a muzzle. Make gathering stitches around the cheek shape, place some polyester stuffing at the centre, pull up the gathering threads and secure them with a knot. Place the cheeks onto the head front, about 1.5cm (⅝ in) under the eyes, and stitch in place. Make the nose in the same way, then place it on top of the cheeks and stitch in place. Stitch a smiley mouth using three strands of embroidery thread (see Mouths page 15).

6 For the hair, use a darning needle to thread short lengths of thick wool along the top seam of the head, then tie each length of wool with a knot to secure them in place. For the boy, thread three lengths of wool at one side of the head, and for the girl add wool all along the top edge, then trim the hair to the required length. To make a bow, take a 5cm (2in) square of contrast fleece, fold in half and pinch together at the centre, then wrap a 1cm (½ in) wide length of fleece around the centre of the bow and secure with fabric glue. Glue or stitch the bow to the girl's head.

2 To make the antennae, fold each antenna shape in half by bringing the long edges together, with right sides facing, then pin and stitch along the long edge and one short edge. Turn each antenna right side out, then tie a knot at each stitched end.

3 To add the antennae and eyes, follow step 3 of the Smiley Faces instructions on page 75, but place each antennae between the black dots. To make the head and lining, follow step 4 of the Smiley Faces instructions.

4 For the nose, make gathering stitches around the nose shape, place some polyester stuffing at the centre, pull up the gathering threads and secure them with a knot. Place the nose under the eyes and stitch in place. Finally, stitch a mouth using embroidery thread (see Mouths page 15).

Alien

Additional materials
• Two safety boggle eyes, 18mm

1 Photocopy the Happy Heads pattern pieces on pages 120–121, then cut out the paper shapes to use as templates. From the fleece cut 2 heads, 2 antennae, 1 base and 1 nose. From the lining cut 1 base and 2 heads.

Little Devil

Additional materials
• Two solid black safety eyes, 11mm
• Scrap of black fleece for nose

1 Photocopy the Happy Heads pattern pieces on pages 120–121, then cut out the paper shapes to use as templates. From the red fleece cut 2 heads, 4 horns and 1 base. From the black fleece cut 1 nose. From the lining fabric cut 1 base and 2 heads.

2 With right sides facing, pin and stitch the horns together in pairs, leaving the bottom edge open, then turn the horns right side out.

3 To add the horns and eyes, follow step 3 of the Smiley Faces instructions on page 75, but match each horn shape to the black dots.

4 To finish the Little Devil, follow step 4 of the Smiley Faces on page 75, and step 4 of the Alien instructions on page 76.

3 To add the ears and eyes, follow step 3 of the Smiley Faces instructions page 75, but match each ear shape to the black dots. To make the head and lining, follow step 4 for the Smiley Faces.

4 To make the muzzle and nose, follow step 5 of the Smiley Faces instructions. Then, use two strands of embroidery thread to make the cheeks and add the whiskers and mouth (see Cheeks and Muzzles page 14 and Whiskers and Mouths page 15).

Cat

Additional materials
• Two safety boggle eyes, 12mm
• Scrap of black fleece for nose
• Scrap of contrast fleece for muzzle and ears

1 Photocopy the Happy Heads pattern pieces on pages 120–121, then cut out the paper shapes to use as templates. From the main fleece cut 2 heads, 2 ears and 1 base. From the contrast fleece cut 2 ears and 1 muzzle. From the black fleece cut 1 nose. From the lining fabric cut 1 base and 2 heads.

2 To make the ears, start with right sides facing and stitch one main fleece and one contrast fleece ear shape together, leaving the bottom edge open. Repeat for the other pair then turn the ears right side out.

Rabbit

Additional materials
• Two safety boggle eyes, 12mm
• Small pink pom-pom for nose
• Scrap of contrast fleece for ears and muzzle

1 Photocopy the Happy Heads pattern pieces on pages 120–121, then cut out the paper shapes to use as templates. From the main fleece cut 2 heads, 2 ears and 1 base. From the contrast fleece cut 2 ears and 1 muzzle. From the lining fabric cut 1 base and 2 heads.

2 To complete your Rabbit follow steps 2–4 of the Cat instructions, but instead of making a fabric nose, simply glue or stitch on a pom-pom.

Dog

Additional materials
• Two amber safety eyes, 14mm
• Scrap of black fleece for nose and ears

1 Photocopy the Happy Heads pattern pieces on pages 120–121, then cut out the paper shapes to use as templates. From the main fleece cut 2 heads, 1 base and 1 muzzle. From the black fleece cut 4 ears and 1 nose. From the lining fabric cut 1 base and 2 heads.

2 With right sides facing, pin and stitch the ears together in pairs, leaving the bottom edge open, then turn the ears right side out.

3 To complete your Dog, follow steps 3 and 4 of the Cat instructions on page 77.

Lion

Additional materials
• Contrast fleece, 20cm (8in) square
• Two amber safety eyes, 10mm
• Small black pom-pom for nose

1 Photocopy the Happy Heads pattern pieces on pages 120–121, then cut out the paper shapes to use as templates. From the main fleece cut 2 heads, 2 ears and 1 base. From the contrast fleece cut 2 ears, 1 muzzle and 1 mane. From the lining fabric cut 1 base and 2 heads.

2 Follow steps 2 and 3 of the Cat instructions on page 77. Cut the slits on the mane as indicated on the pattern, then pin the mane centrally onto the head front. Use slipstitches to stitch the inner edge of the mane to the face, making a 6mm (¼in) turning as you go.

3 To complete your Lion follow step 4 of the Cat instructions on page 77, but instead of making a fabric nose, simply glue or stitch on a pom-pom.

Frog

Additional materials
• Yellow fleece, 10 x 15cm (4 x 6in)
• Two safety boggle eyes, 18mm

1 Photocopy the Happy Heads pattern pieces on pages 120–121, then cut out the paper shapes to use as templates. From the main fleece cut 1 head, 1 upper face and 1 base. From the yellow fleece cut 1 lower face. From the lining fabric cut 1 base and 2 heads.

2 With right sides facing, pin and stitch the upper and lower face shapes together,

matching the white dots. Add the two safety boggle eyes to the head front in the positions indicated on the pattern (see Safety Eyes and Noses page 16).

3 To make the head and lining, follow step 4 for the Smiley Faces on page 75, then stitch a mouth using embroidery thread (see Mouths page 15).

TINY HAPPY HEADS

● ●

To make each tiny Happy Head, use the pattern pieces on pages 120–121, reducing the patterns on a photocopier by 50%. (You could use the grid method described on page 10 to reduce the patterns by half but photocopying is easier.) Follow the instructions for each large Happy Head character, but use stick-on boggle eyes or add embroidered French knots for eyes. Because the tiny heads are so small, you do not need to add lining.

Fridge Magnets, Badges and Zipper Friends
If you want to make your tiny Happy Heads into fridge magnets, simply glue a craft magnet to the back of the head. To make a badge, stitch or glue a brooch clip to the back of the head. To make a 'zipper friend', stitch a quick-release swivel hook to the top of the head.

Hair Scrunchie
To make a hair scrunchie, either stitch a tiny Happy Head to an existing scrunchie, or make your own. Cut a 7.5 x 30cm (3 x 12in) length of fleece and a 25cm (10in) length of elastic. With right sides facing, fold the fleece in half along the length, stitch along the length, then turn right side out to make a tube. Thread the elastic through the tube and stitch the elastic ends together to form a loop. On the fleece tube, turn a 6mm (¼in) hem at one end, then insert the raw edges of the other end under the hem and stitch in place. Stitch a tiny Happy Head to the top edge of the scrunchie.

JUGGLING BABIES

This collection of bean bag babies from around the world are all made from the same simple pattern, with babies of different nationalities created by changing the colour of the head, hair or eyes, and using different body fabrics like ethnic prints, stars and stripes or Chinese silks. You could add different shaped eyes, bindi spots, or different shaped hats to accentuate the characteristics of each nationality. The babies are the ideal size to hold in your hand and as they are filled with plastic beans, they are the perfect weight to use as juggling balls. You could make groups of different characters or co-ordinated sets of juggling babies as gifts. Make them look like friends or family, dress them in school uniform colours, or make clowns and other characters.

Babies From Around the World

What you will need for each baby
- Fleece for the head, 20cm (8in) square
- Body fabric, 30 x 40cm (12 x 16in)
- Lining fabric, 30cm (12in) square
- Polyester stuffing for filling
- Plastic beans
- Matching sewing thread
- Embroidery thread for eyes

1 You will find the Juggling Babies pattern pieces on page 122. Only half of the head, base and body shapes are shown. To make a whole pattern shape, either photocopy the shapes twice, cut them out and stick them together, or trace the shapes onto paper, fold the paper along the fold line indicated on the pattern and cut around the shape. Refer to Cutting Out on page 11 if necessary.

2 Use the paper templates to cut out the fabric pieces. From the fleece cut 1 head. From the body fabric cut 1 body base and 2 bodies. From the lining fabric cut 1 body base and 2 rectangles 10 x 18cm (4 x 7in).

3 Make gathering stitches around the fleece head shape, 1.5cm (⅝in) from the edge. Place a ball of polyester stuffing at the centre, pull up the gathering threads and secure them with a knot to form a head and neck. To make the nose, make a small circle of running stitches on the head front, gently pull up the threads to form a nose shape, then secure the threads with a knot. Work two small French knots using embroidery thread for the eyes.

4 With right sides facing, pin and stitch the body shapes together along the side edges. Clip into the corners above and below each arm. With right sides facing, pin and stitch the base to the lower edge of the body shape, matching the side seams with the black dots on the base, then turn the body right side out. Fold a 1cm (½in) hem along the neck edge of the body, then make a row a gathering stitches along this edge.

5 To make the lining bag, pin and stitch the lining body shapes together along the short sides. Pin and stitch the base to the lower edge of the body shape, matching the side seams with the black dots on the base. Turn the lining bag right side out. Make a row of gathering stitches around the top edge of the bag. Half fill the lining bag with plastic beans, then pull up the gathering threads tightly and secure them with a knot, then insert the lining bag into the body.

6 To attach the head to the body, place the neck edge of the head inside the neck edge of the body. Pull up the gathering threads, so that the top edge of the body fabric gathers around the neck. Secure the head to the body with slip-stitches around the neck and fabric gathers.

To Make Hair

Use a darning needle to thread short lengths of thick wool along the top of the head. Tie each length of wool with a knot to secure and trim to length.

African Hat: Using a suitable ethic-print fabric, cut 1 African hat base and 1 strip 2.5 x 14cm (1 x 5½in) for the hat brim. With right sides facing, fold the strip in half so the short edges meet, then stitch the short edges together. With wrong sides facing, fold the strip in half along the length and press the fold in place. With right sides facing, pin and stitch the hat base to the hat brim, matching all the raw edges. Turn the hat right side out and secure to the head with slipstitches.

To Make Hats

Clown Hat: Cut 1 clown hat shape from felt. Fold the hat shape in half so the two straight edges meet, then stitch the straight edges together. Turn the hat right side out, stitch a pom-pom at the tip and stitch ric-rac braid around the bottom edge. Secure to the head with slipstitches.

Scottish Hat: Cut 1 Scottish hat shape from tartan fabric. Make gathering stitches around the hat edge, pull up the gathering threads so the gathered edge meets at the centre of the circle, then secure the threads with a knot. Stitch a pom-pom at the centre of the hat to cover up the gathered edge, then slipstitch the hat to the head.

HANGING AROUND

These cute calico dolls are 30cm (12in) long from hand to toe and have long elasticated arms so you can hang them on door knobs or hooks. They are ideal for children to make as they are made from inexpensive calico, using a very simple pattern shape and fabric marker pens to draw on the faces and clothes. Children could draw members of their family, or even a doll wearing their school uniform. These dolls also make ideal gifts for adults – you could personalise them by writing a name or a message on the tummy, make one for a special occasion, like a wedding doll, fill a doll with pot-pourri to hang inside a wardrobe or cupboard, or make an angel with calico wings. For special friends you could make hobby dolls, such as a sewing friend to hang on a sewing machine, with flowers drawn to look like embroidery stitches and tape measure markings on the legs.

Calico Doll

What you will need

- Calico, 30cm (12in) square
- Polyester lining fabric, 20 x 30cm (8 x 12in)
- Selection of fabric marker pens
- Elastic, 6mm (¼in) wide x 30cm (12in) long
- Polyester stuffing for filling
- Plastic beans
- Matching sewing thread

1 Photocopy the Hanging Around pattern pieces on page 123 and cut out the paper shapes to use as templates. From the calico cut 2 bodies, 4 legs, and 1 strip for the arms 6 x 54cm (2¼ x 21in). From the lining fabric cut 2 bodies. Refer to Cutting Out page 11 if necessary.

2 Place one of the body shapes right side up on a hard flat surface, then following the

manufacturer's instructions, use fabric marker pens to draw the face and clothes. Do the same with two of the legs if you want to draw shoes, socks or anything on them. Iron the fabric shapes from the wrong side to fix the pen and to make it washable.

3 With right sides facing, pin and stitch the legs together in pairs, leaving the top edge open. Turn right side out and add a small amount of stuffing to each.

4 For the arms, fold the long strip in half along the length so the edges meet. Pin and stitch the strip along the length to make a tube, then turn the tube right side out. Thread the elastic through the tube and secure the elastic ends at each end of the tube with hand stitches. Tie a knot at the centre of the tube to make the hands.

5 Place the arms over the body front, between the white dots, so that they face inwards and all the raw edges meet. Pin and tack (baste) in place, then do the same with the legs, placing them between the black dots.

6 With right sides facing, pin and stitch the two body shapes together, sandwiching the arms and legs on the inside and leaving a gap at the base, then turn right side out. Repeat this process for the lining bag (without the arms and legs). Lightly fill the head with polyester stuffing and the tummy with plastic beans, then secure the gap with slipstitches. Insert the lining bag into the body, then secure the gap at the body base with slipstitches.

7 Finally, stitch any ribbon bows, buttons or trimmings on the doll to add character.

Calico Angel

What you will need

- Calico, 30 x 40cm (12 x 16in)
- Polyester lining fabric, 20 x 30cm (8 x 12in)
- Selection of fabric marker pens
- Elastic, 6mm (¼in) wide x 30cm (12in) long
- Polyester stuffing for filling
- Plastic beans
- Matching sewing thread
- Thin gold ribbon, 1m (1⅛yd) long
- Three gold star sequins

1 Photocopy the Hanging Around pattern pieces on page 123, then cut out the paper shapes to use as templates. From the calico cut 2 bodies, 4 legs, 2 wings and 1 strip for the arms 6 x 54cm (2¼ x 21in). From the lining fabric cut 2 bodies.

2 To make the Calico Angel, follow steps 2–6 of the Calico Doll.

3 To make the wing, with right sides facing, pin and stitch the two wing shapes together, leaving a gap at the base. Turn right side out and secure the gap with slipstitches. Press the wings then make a row of machine stitches all around the edge of the wings.

4 Cut a 60cm (24in) length of gold ribbon, fold in half to find the centre then stitch the centre of the ribbon to the angel wings at the black dot. Place the wings at the back of the angel then bring both ends of the ribbon to the front of the body, above the arms. To tie the wings in place, cross both ribbon ends over the chest, take them around the body back, cross over and bring back to the front, then tie in a bow at the waist.

5 To finish the angel, make a halo by tying a length of gold ribbon around the head and stitching a gold star sequin at the front of the ribbon. Tie a length of gold ribbon around each ankle and stitch a gold star sequin at the front of the ribbon on each ankle.

HAPPY HALLOWE'EN

This spooky bunch of bean bag friends might think they look scary but really they're quite cute. The bat, ghost and pumpkin are all based on the same triangular body shape, with the addition of arms, ears, wings and feet. The cat is made from an elongated triangle with ears and a tail. The spooky creatures sitting on the broomstick are made as toys. The bat, ghost and pumpkin are 15cm (6in) tall and the cat is 25cm (10in) tall. Smaller versions of the creatures have been made to decorate a Hallowe'en wreath on page 93 and these measure 10cm (4in) and 15cm (6in) tall, though you could reduce the patterns to a size of your choice. A selection of fur, fleece and sparkly Lycra have been used to give each creature a different character.

Black Cat

What you will need
- Black luxury velour, 40cm (16in) square
- Black fleece, 15cm (6in) square
- Polyester lining fabric, 40cm (16in) square
- Pink pom-pom
- Thin elastic, 13cm (5in) long
- Two safety boggle eyes, 12mm
- Polyester stuffing for filling
- Plastic beans
- Matching sewing thread
- Grey embroidery thread for whiskers

1 Photocopy the Happy Hallowe'en pattern pieces on pages 124–125, then cut out the paper shapes to use as templates. From the black velour cut 1 cat tail, 2 cat ears and 2 cat bodies. From the black fleece cut 2 cat ears and 1 cat muzzle. From the lining fabric cut 2 cat bodies. Refer to Cutting Out on page 11 if necessary.

2 To make the ears, pin and stitch one fur and one fleece ear shape together, right sides facing, leaving the bottom edge open. Repeat for the other pair then turn both ears right side out.

3 To make the tail, fold the tail shape in half by bringing the long edges together with right sides facing, then pin and stitch along the long edge and one short edge. Stretch the elastic along the long edge, stitch in place along the stitching line, then turn the tail right side out.

4 Place the ears fleece side down, over the body front so that they face inwards, matching the black dots so that all the raw edges meet. Pin and tack (baste) the ears in place, then do the same for the tail, placing it between the dotted lines shown on the pattern. Add the two safety eyes to the cat body front in

the positions indicated by the two circles on the pattern (see Safety Eyes and Noses page 16).

5 To make the body, pin and stitch the two body shapes together, right sides facing, leaving a gap at the base. Turn right side out. Repeat this process to make the lining bag. Lightly fill the lining bag with polyester stuffing and plastic beans, then secure the gap with slip-stitches. Insert the lining bag into the cat body, then secure the gap at the body base with slip-stitches.

6 For the muzzle, make gathering stitches around the fleece muzzle shape, place some stuffing at the centre, pull up the gathering threads and secure them with a knot. Place the muzzle onto the body front, under the eyes and stitch in place. Use matching sewing thread to make the cheeks (see Cheeks and Muzzles page 14), then use two strands of embroidery thread to stitch the whiskers. Finally, glue or stitch the pink pom-pom nose in place.

Sparkly Bat

• •

What you will need
- Sparkly Lycra, 50cm (20in) square
- Scraps of black felt for feet
- Polyester lining fabric, 30cm (12in) square
- Two safety boggle eyes, 12mm
- Polyester stuffing for filling
- Plastic beans
- Matching sewing thread

1 Photocopy the Happy Hallowe'en pattern pieces on pages 124–125, then cut out the paper shapes to use as templates. From the sparkly Lycra cut 4 bat ears, 4 bat wings, 1 nose and 2 bodies. From the black felt cut 2 bat feet. From the lining fabric cut 2 bodies.

2 With right sides facing, pin and stitch two ear shapes together, leaving the bottom edge open. Repeat for the other pair then turn the ears right side out. Do the same with each pair of wings, stitching around the curved edges, leaving the side edges open, and then turning the wings right side out. Machine stitch around the curved edges and through the centre of each wing, along the dotted lines indicated on the pattern.

3 Place the ears over the body front so that they face inwards, matching the black squares so that all the raw edges meet. Pin and tack (baste) the ears in place. Repeat this process for the wings, matching the black dots at the body sides, then do the same for the feet at the body base, placing them between the dotted lines. Add the two safety eyes to the body front in the positions indicated on the pattern (see Safety Eyes and Noses page 16).

4 To make the bat body and lining bag, follow step 5 of the Black Cat instructions page 89.

5 For the nose, make gathering stitches around the nose shape, place some stuffing at the centre, pull up the gathering threads and secure them with a knot. Place the nose on to the body front, under the eyes, and stitch in place (see Noses page 14).

Happy Ghost

• •

What you will need
- White fleece, 30cm (12in) square
- Polyester lining fabric, 30cm (12in) square
- Two safety boggle eyes, 12mm
- Polyester stuffing for filling
- Plastic beans
- Matching sewing thread
- Black and white embroidery thread

1 Photocopy the Happy Hallowe'en pattern pieces on pages 124–125, then cut out the paper shapes to use as templates. From the white fleece cut 4 ghost arms, 1 nose and 2 bodies. From the lining fabric cut 2 bodies.

2 With right sides facing, pin and stitch two arm shapes together, leaving the top edge open. Repeat for the other pair then turn the arms right side out. Lightly fill the hands with polyester stuffing, then use the white embroidery thread to add the fingers (see Fingers and Toes page 15).

3 Place the arms over the body front so that they face inwards, matching the white dots so that all the raw edges meet. Pin and tack (baste) the arms in place. Add the two safety eyes to the body front in the positions indicated on the pattern (see Safety Eyes and Noses page 16).

4 Follow step 5 of the Black Cat instructions on page 89, and then step 5 for the Sparkly Bat on page 90. Stitch the mouth using two strands of black embroidery thread (see Mouths page 15).

Pumpkin Pal

What you will need

- Orange fleece, 30cm (12in) square
- Green fleece, 25cm (10in) square
- Scrap of brown felt for nose
- Polyester lining fabric, 30cm (12in) square
- Two safety boggle eyes, 12mm
- Polyester stuffing for filling
- Plastic beans
- Matching sewing thread
- Brown embroidery thread

1 Photocopy the Happy Hallowe'en pattern pieces on pages 124–125, then cut out the paper shapes to use as templates. From the green fleece cut 2 leaves and 1 stalk. From the orange fleece cut 2 bodies. From the brown felt cut 1 nose. From the lining fabric cut 2 bodies.

2 With right sides facing, pin and stitch the leaf shapes together leaving a gap for turning. Turn right side out, then machine stitch around the edge of the leaf shape. Roll the stalk shape into a cylinder, then stitch the long edge in place (see Rolled Cylinders page 16). Stitch the stalk to the centre of the leaf shape.

3 Follow step 5 of the Black Cat instructions on page 89, and then step 5 for the Sparkly Bat on page 90. Stitch the mouth using two strands of brown embroidery thread (see Mouths page 15).

4 Make the lines at the sides of the pumpkin in running stitch using six strands of embroidery thread in your needle. On either side of the pumpkin face, make two rows of running stitches around the front and back of the pumpkin body, starting and finishing at the top edge. Pull up the running stitches to make the body slightly wrinkled, secure the threads with a knot, then hide the knots by stitching the leaf to the top of the pumpkin.

Hallowe'en Wreath

• •

What you will need

- Wire coat-hanger
- Polyester wadding (batting), 0.3m x 150cm (⅜ yd x 60in) wide
- Black polyester lining fabric, 0.5m x 115cm (⅝ yd x 45in) wide
- Silver stars
- Thin black ribbon
- Bundles of twigs
- PVA glue

1 Reduce the Happy Hallowe'en pattern pieces on pages 124–125 on a photocopier by 75% and then cut out the paper shapes to use as templates. (You could use the grid method described on page 10 to reduce the patterns but photocopying is easier.)

2 Follow the instructions for the cat, bat, ghost and pumpkin on the previous pages, using fabrics of your choice. Each bean bag character is made in exactly the same way, only smaller.

3 To make the wreath, carefully bend the coat-hanger into a circular shape, with the hook at the top. Next, wind the thin black ribbon around the coat-hanger hook until it is completely covered and glue the ends of the ribbon in place.

4 To add the padding to the wreath, cut the polyester wadding (batting) along its length into 7.5cm (3in) wide strips, then wind the strips all around the coat-hanger to the required thickness, stitching or gluing the ends in place. Repeat the process with the polyester lining fabric, winding it around the wreath until all the padding is covered.

5 Glue silver stars over the front of the wreath, then tie two small bundles of twigs together with black ribbon. Use the ribbon to tie one bundle at the top and one at the bottom of the wreath. Stitch or glue the small bat to the top of the wreath, then hang the wreath in place and sit the cat, ghost and pumpkin snugly inside the bottom curve.

CHRISTMAS CAPERS

This colourful bunch of characters are sure to add a touch of festive cheer at Christmas time. The Christmas tree, snowman and reindeer stand 18cm (7in) tall and are all based on the same simple pattern, whilst the small yellow star with its Christmas hat, measures 13cm (5in) across. For fun, you could reduce the pattern pieces to make miniature versions as tree decorations. Follow the instructions for the larger versions, but add stick-on boggle eyes, pom-pom noses, and thread a hanging loop at the top. For even more festive cheer, enlarge the pattern to make a giant Christmas advent tree with a sparkly star on top (see page 126 for the enlargement percentage). Stitch twenty-five lengths of ribbon at random over the tree front, so that shinny brass bells can be tied all over it with ribbon bows.

BASIC CHRISTMAS CHARACTERS

Listed below are the basic materials needed to make the characters, with any extra materials needed listed separately under each character.

What you will need for each Christmas character

- Fleece (green, beige or white), 30cm (12in) square
- Polyester lining fabric, 30cm (12in) square
- Polyester stuffing for filling
- Plastic beans
- Matching sewing thread

Christmas Tree

Additional materials
- Two safety boggle eyes, 12mm
- Sparkly green braid, 60cm (¾yd)
- One large gold pom-pom
- Fifteen small sparkly pom-poms

1 Photocopy the Christmas Capers pattern pieces on page 126, then cut out the paper shapes to use as templates. From the green fleece cut 2 bodies, 4 arms and 1 nose. From the lining fabric cut 2 bodies. Refer to Cutting Out on page 11 if necessary.

2 To make the arms, start with right sides facing and pin and stitch the arms together in pairs, leaving the top edge open. Turn right side out and add a small amount of stuffing to each arm.

3 Add the eyes to the body front in the positions indicated by the two circles on the pattern (see Safety Eyes and Noses page 16). Place the arms over the body front so that they

face inwards, matching the black dots so that all the raw edges meet. Pin and tack (baste) in place.

4 To make the body, with right sides facing, pin and stitch the two body shapes together, leaving a gap at the base, then turn right side out. Repeat this process to make the lining bag. Lightly fill the bag with polyester stuffing and plastic beans, then secure the gap with slip-stitches. Insert the lining bag into the body, then secure the gap at the body base with slipstitches.

5 Make gathering stitches around the nose shape, place some stuffing at the centre, pull up the gathering threads and secure them with a knot. Stitch the nose onto the body front (see Noses page 14).

6 Finally, pin and stitch the green sparkly braid to the body front in a zigzag pattern. Stitch the large sparkly pom-pom at the top of the tree and the small ones randomly over the tree front.

Red-Nosed Reindeer

• •

Additional materials

- Dark brown fleece, 10 x 25cm (4 x 10in)
- Scrap of red fleece for nose
- Scraps of green felt for leaves
- Two safety boggle eyes, 12mm
- One small red pom-pom
- One brass bell, 18mm
- Green ribbon, 20cm (8in) long

1 Photocopy the Christmas Capers pattern pieces on page 126, then cut out the paper shapes to use as templates. From the beige fleece cut 2 bodies. From the dark brown fleece cut 4 antlers. From the red fleece cut 1 nose. From the green felt cut 2 holly leaves. From the lining fabric cut 2 bodies.

2 To make the antlers, follow step 2 of the Christmas Tree arm instructions, matching the antlers together in pairs. Then follow step 3 of the Christmas Tree instructions, but matching the white dots.

3 Follow steps 4 and 5 of the Christmas Tree instructions. Finally, stitch the felt holly leaves and small red pom-pom to the top of the reindeer's head, and the ribbon bow and brass bell to the lower body.

Snowman

• •

Additional materials

- Scraps of dark brown fleece for arms
- Scrap of orange fleece for nose
- Red fleece for scarf, 2.5 x 40cm (1 x 16in)
- Two black ball safety eyes, 11mm
- Two tiny black pom-poms

1 Photocopy the Christmas Capers pattern pieces on page 126, then cut out the paper shapes as templates. From the white fleece cut 2 bodies. From the dark brown fleece cut 2 snowman arms. From the orange fleece cut 1 snowman nose. From the lining fabric cut 2 bodies.

2 Cut the fingers at the end of each arm as indicated by the lines on the pattern. Roll each arm into a cylinder, then stitch the long edge in place (see Rolled Cylinders page 16).

3 Follow steps 3 and 4 of the Christmas Tree instructions on page 96, placing the arms between the black dots for step 3.

4 Fold the nose cone in half so that the two straight edges meet and stitch them together.

Turn the nose right side out. Make small gathering stitches all around the nose top, pull up the threads, then wind them tightly around the length of the nose and secure them with a knot (see picture on page 96). Stitch the nose to the body front.

5 Cut a fringe at each end of the red fleece scarf and tie the scarf in place around the neck. Finally, glue or stitch two tiny black pompoms to the body front.

Bright Star

· ·

What you will need

- Yellow fleece 15 x 30cm (6 x 12in)
- Red fleece, 13cm (5in) square
- Polyester lining fabric, 15 x 30cm (6 x 12in)
- Two stick-on boggle eyes, 10mm
- White ric-rac braid, 13cm (5in) long
- One small white pom-pom
- Polyester stuffing for filling
- Plastic beans
- Matching sewing thread
- Embroidery thread

1 Photocopy the Christmas Capers pattern pieces on page 126, then cut out the paper shapes to use as templates. From the yellow fleece cut 2 star bodies and 1 star nose. From the red fleece cut 2 triangles each 6.5 x 10 x 10cm (2½ x 4 x 4in). From the lining fabric cut 2 star bodies.

2 With right sides facing, pin and stitch the hat pieces together, leaving the bottom edge open, then turn right side out. Turn under a 6mm (¼in) hem, stitch ric-rac braid along the bottom edge, then stitch a small white pompom to the tip of the hat.

3 Add the stick-on eyes to the body front, then, follow steps 4 and 5 of the Christmas Tree instructions on page 96.

4 Use three strands of embroidery thread to add a mouth using backstitch (see Mouths page 15). Finally, place the hat over the top point of the star, stitch the lower hat edge in place, bend over the hat tip and secure in place with a few hand stitches.

PATTERNS

● ●

The patterns provided on the following pages will enable you to make any of the bean bag characters in the book; you could also adapt them to create designs of your own. Nearly all the patterns are provided actual size so all you need to do is photocopy or trace them onto paper, then cut out the pieces to use as templates. In a few cases the patterns will need enlarging or reducing so you can make the very large or tiny bean bag projects – simply enlarge or reduce the patterns using the grid method on page 10 or on a photocopier using the percentage given in the project instructions. Occasionally patterns overlap to save space.

Wild Things

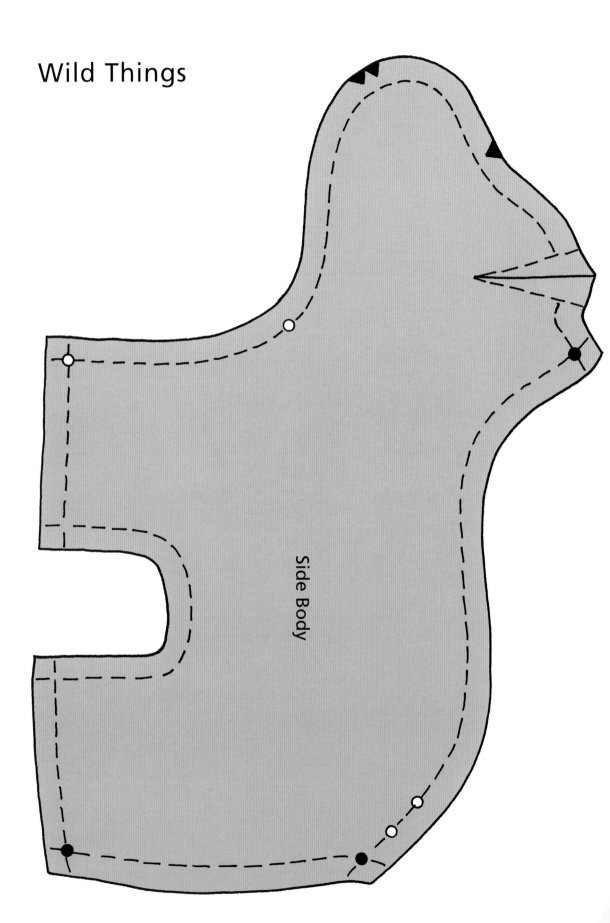

Side Body

Wild Things

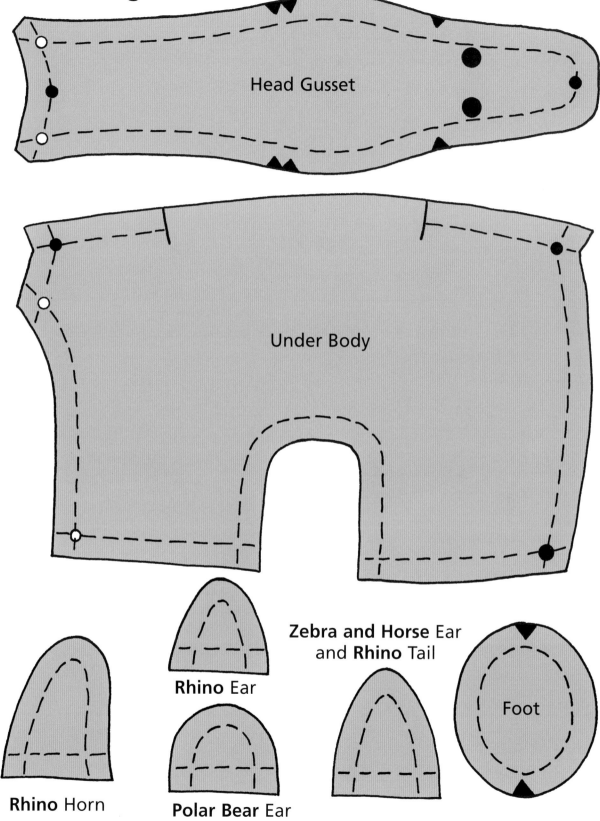

Head Gusset

Under Body

Rhino Ear

Zebra and Horse Ear
and **Rhino** Tail

Foot

Rhino Horn

Polar Bear Ear

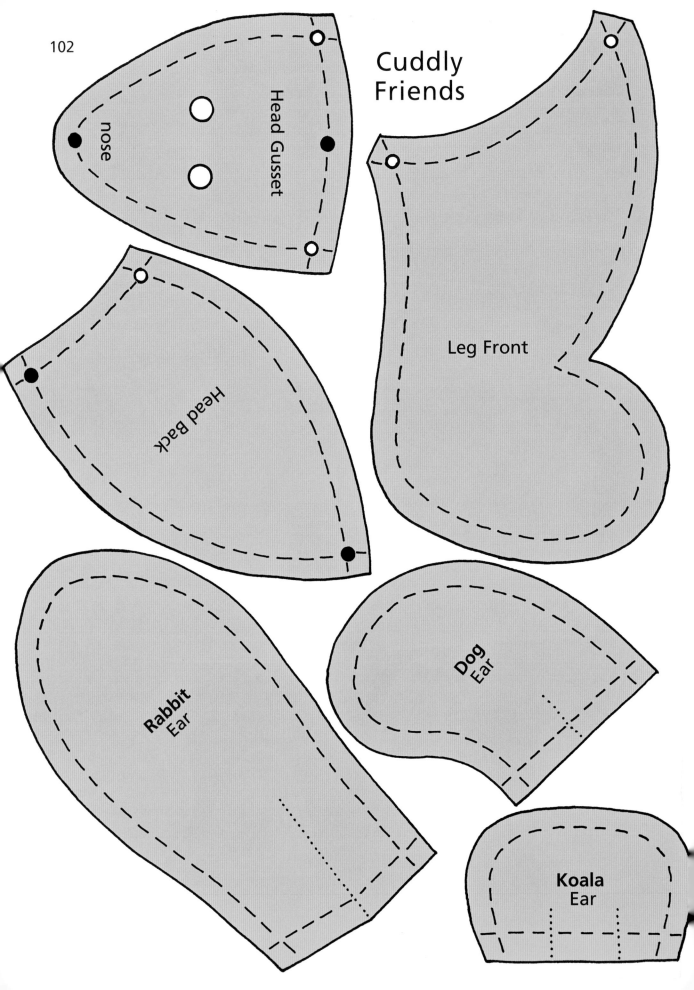

Cuddly
Friends

Head Gusset

nose

Leg Front

Head Back

Rabbit
Ear

Dog
Ear

Koala
Ear

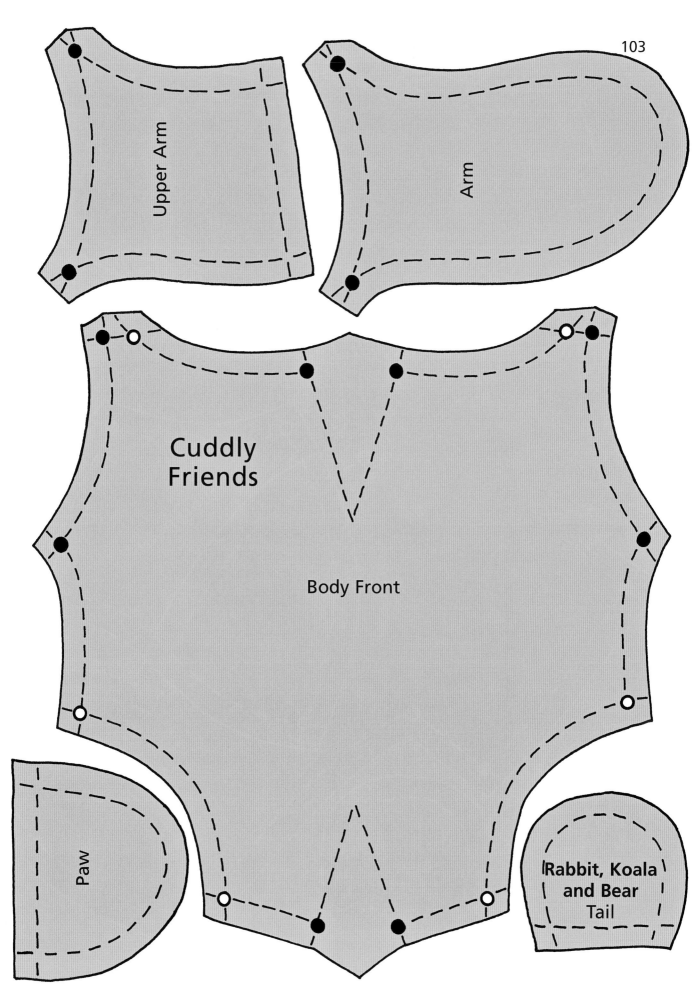

Upper Arm

Arm

Cuddly
Friends

Body Front

Paw

Rabbit, Koala
and Bear
Tail

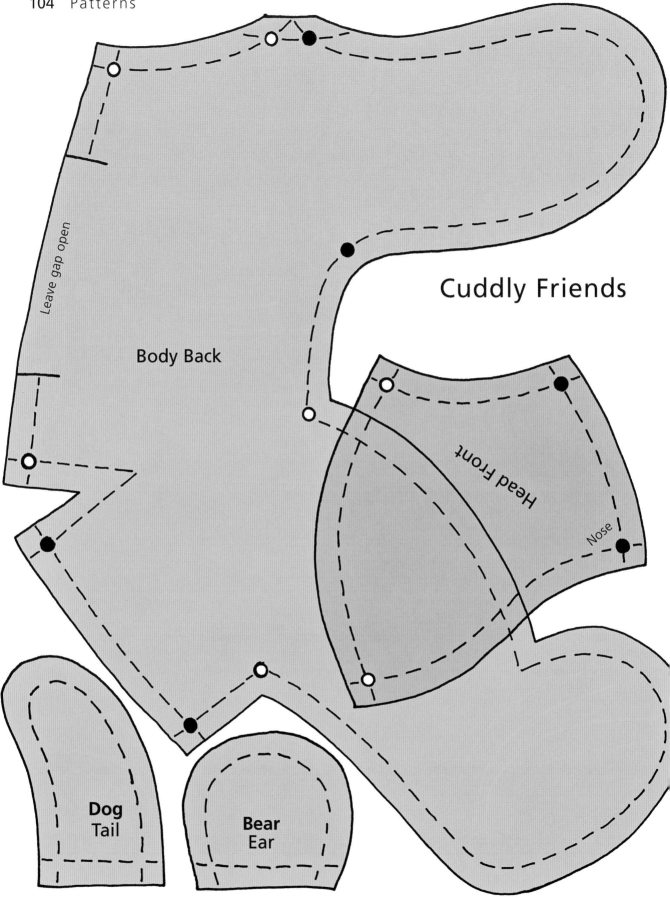

Leave gap open

Body Back

Cuddly Friends

Head Front

Nose

Dog
Tail

Bear
Ear

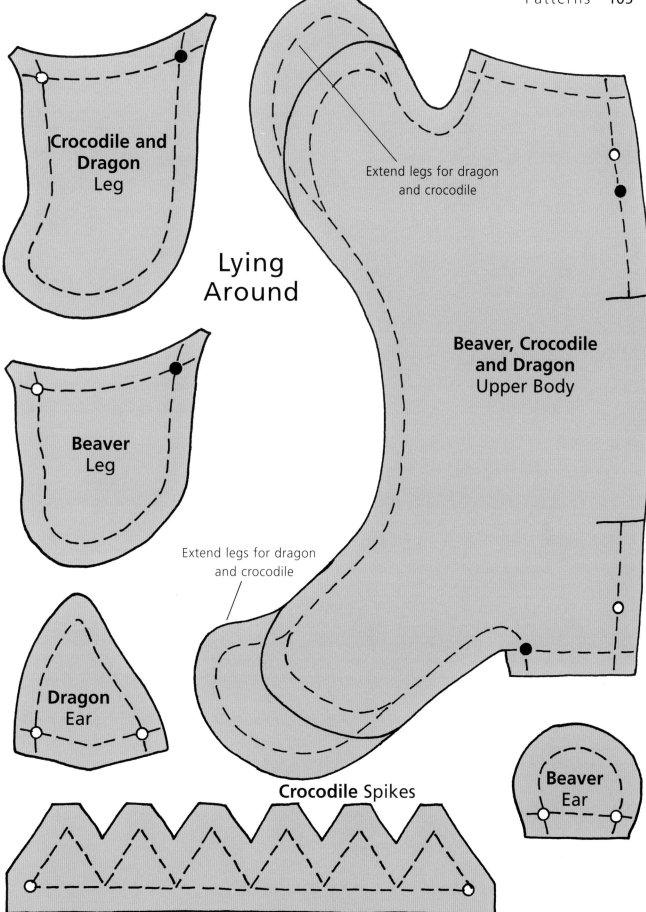

Crocodile and Dragon Leg

Lying Around

Extend legs for dragon and crocodile

Beaver, Crocodile and Dragon Upper Body

Beaver Leg

Extend legs for dragon and crocodile

Dragon Ear

Crocodile Spikes

Beaver Ear

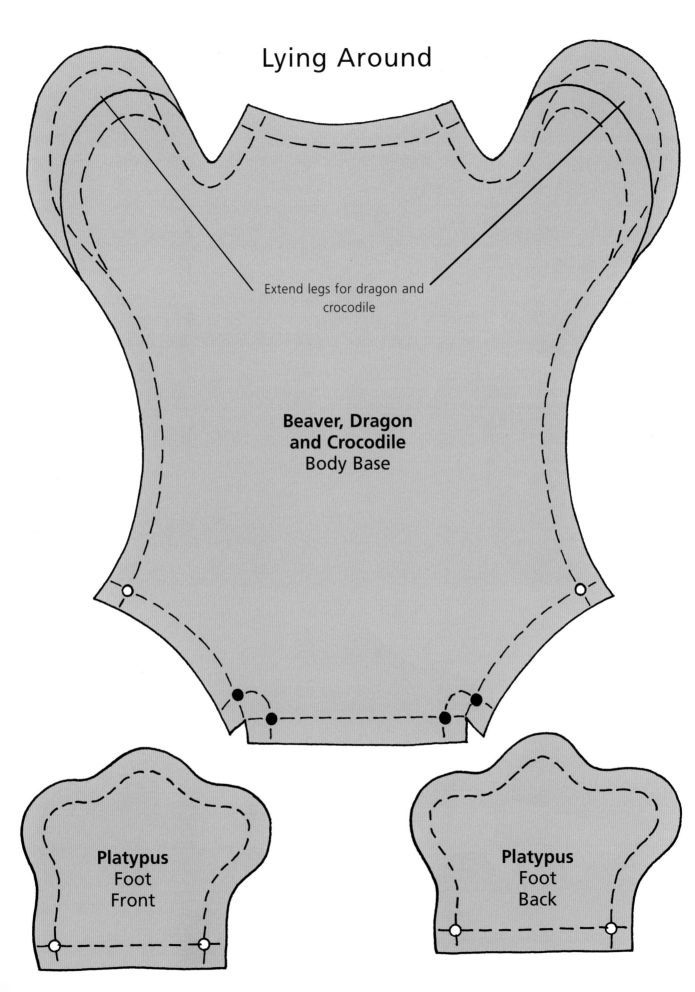

Lying Around

Extend legs for dragon and crocodile

Beaver, Dragon and Crocodile Body Base

Platypus Foot Front

Platypus Foot Back

Lying Around

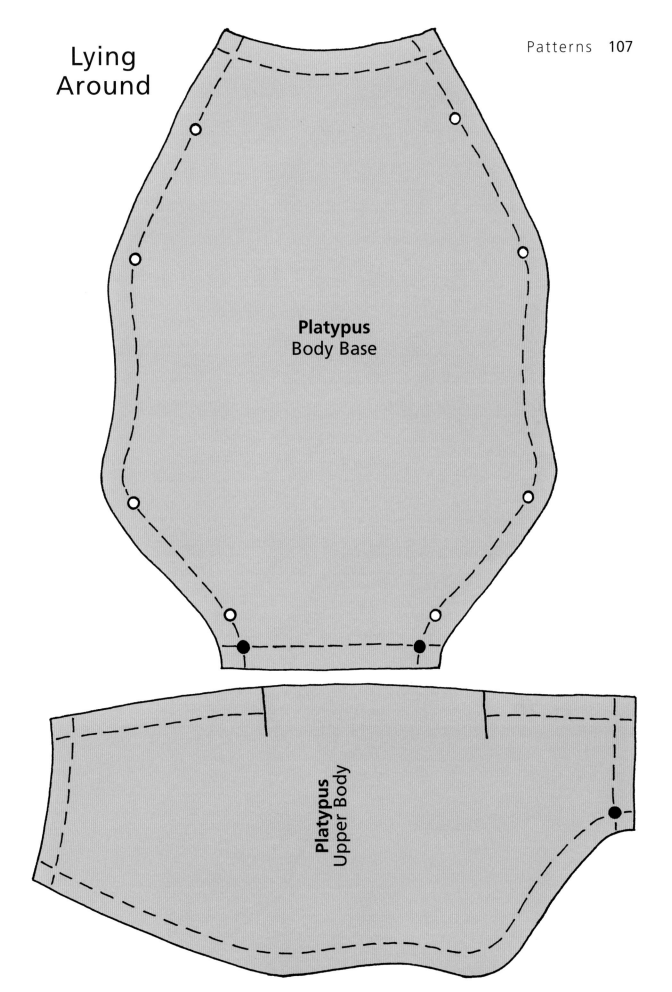

Platypus
Body Base

Platypus
Upper Body

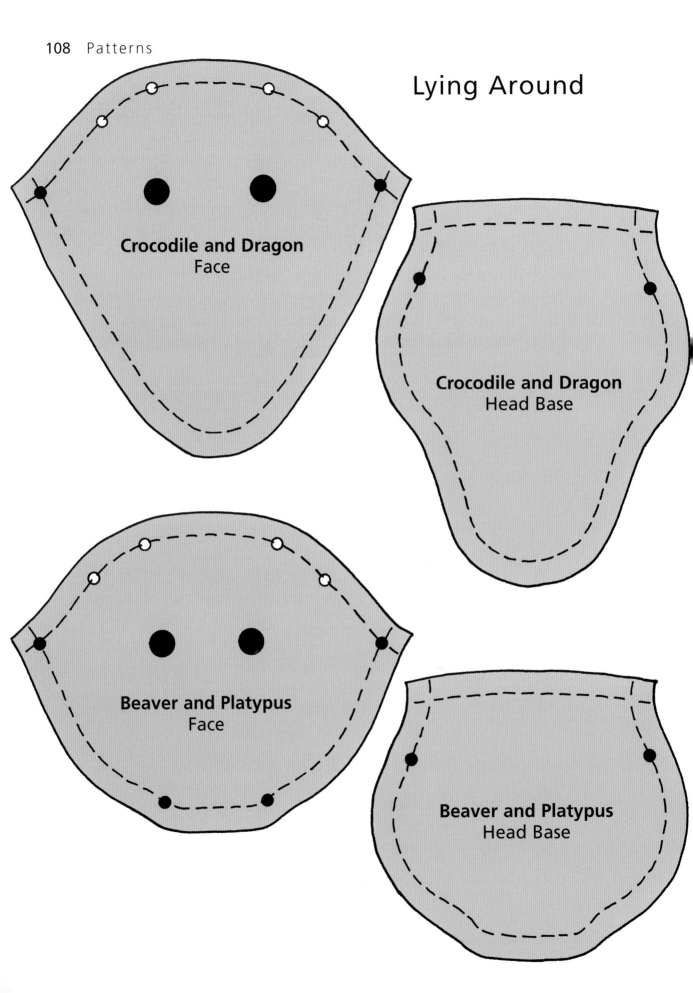

Lying Around

Crocodile and Dragon
Face

Crocodile and Dragon
Head Base

Beaver and Platypus
Face

Beaver and Platypus
Head Base

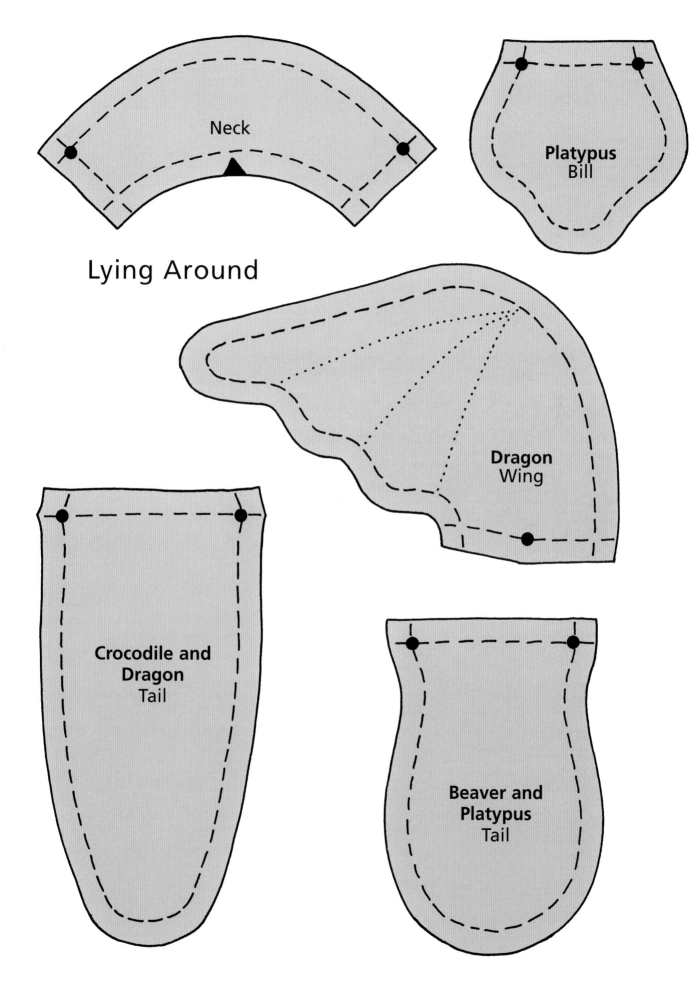

Neck

Lying Around

Platypus
Bill

Dragon
Wing

**Crocodile and
Dragon**
Tail

**Beaver and
Platypus**
Tail

Cheeky
Creatures

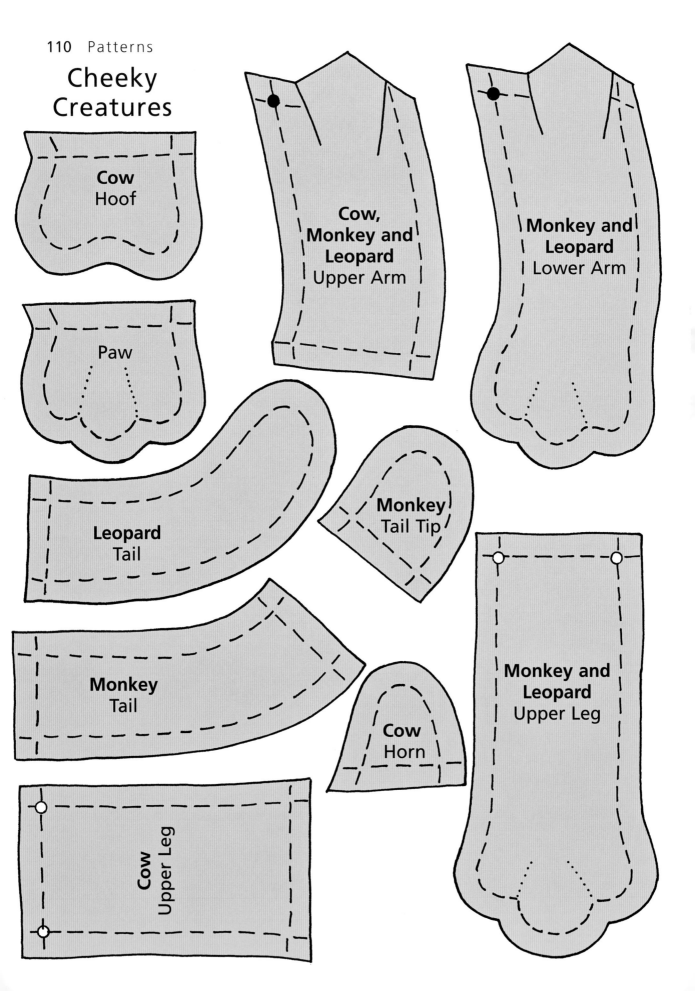

Cow
Hoof

**Cow,
Monkey and
Leopard**
Upper Arm

**Monkey and
Leopard**
Lower Arm

Paw

**Leopard
Tail**

**Monkey
Tail Tip**

**Monkey
Tail**

**Monkey and
Leopard**
Upper Leg

**Cow
Horn**

Cow
Upper Leg

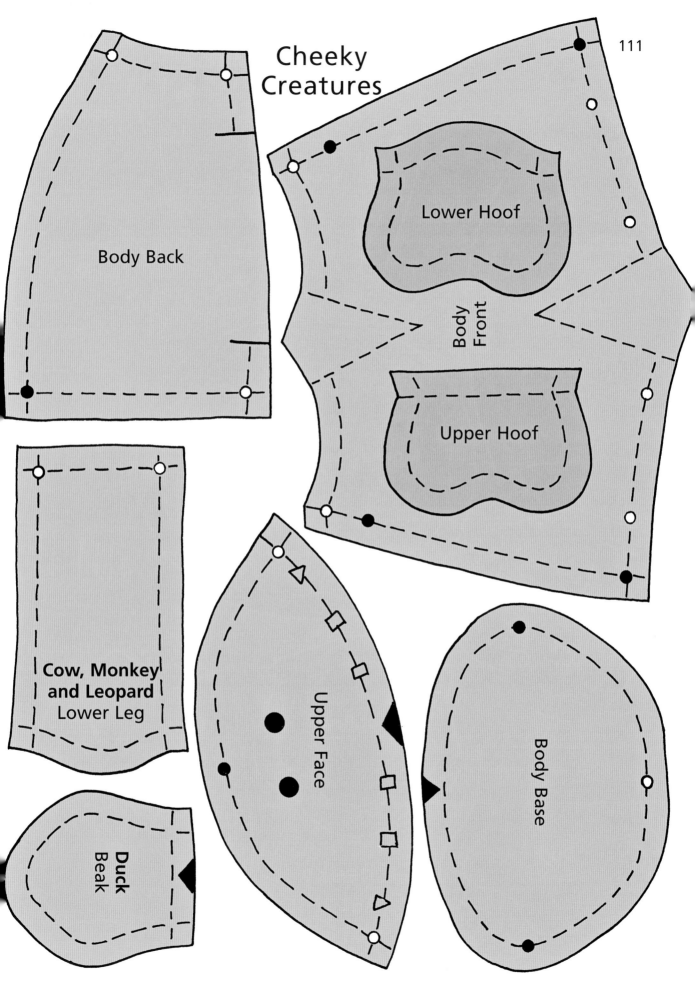

Cheeky Creatures

111

Body Back

Lower Hoof

Body Front

Upper Hoof

Cow, Monkey and Leopard Lower Leg

Upper Face

Body Base

Duck Beak

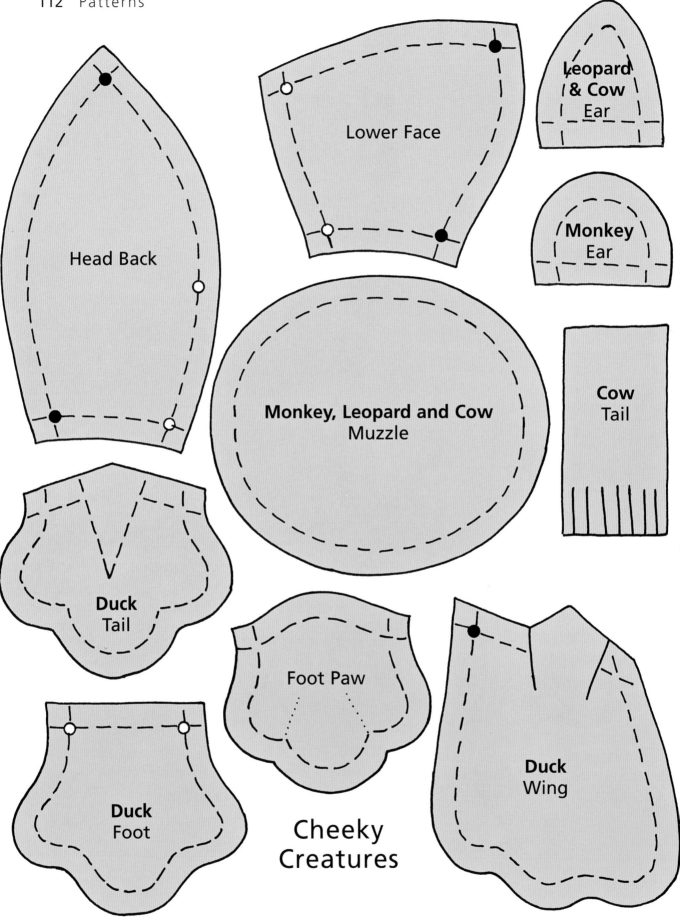

Head Back

Lower Face

Leopard & Cow
Ear

Monkey
Ear

Monkey, Leopard and Cow
Muzzle

Cow
Tail

Duck
Tail

Foot Paw

Duck
Wing

Duck
Foot

Cheeky
Creatures

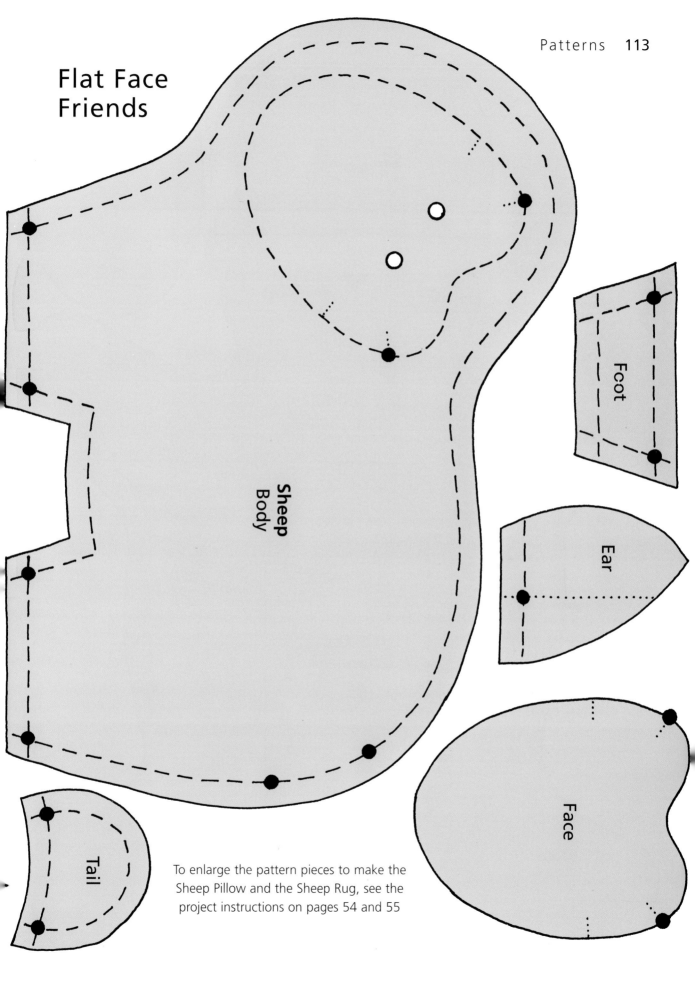

Flat Face Friends

Sheep
Body

Foot

Ear

Face

Tail

To enlarge the pattern pieces to make the
Sheep Pillow and the Sheep Rug, see the
project instructions on pages 54 and 55

Flatties

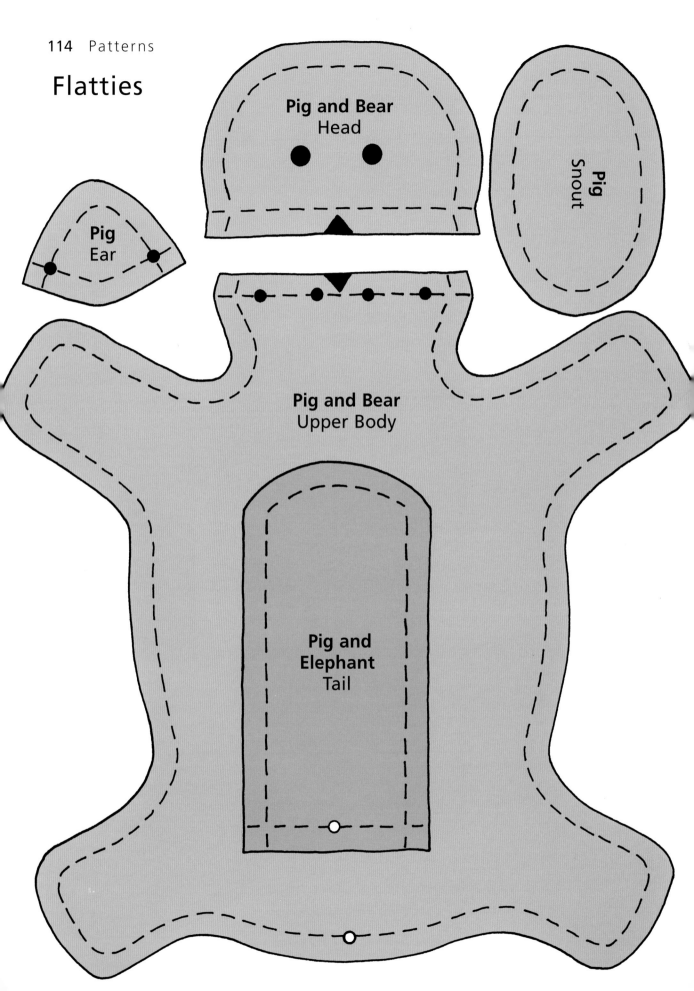

Pig and Bear
Head

Pig
Snout

Pig
Ear

Pig and Bear
Upper Body

Pig and
Elephant
Tail

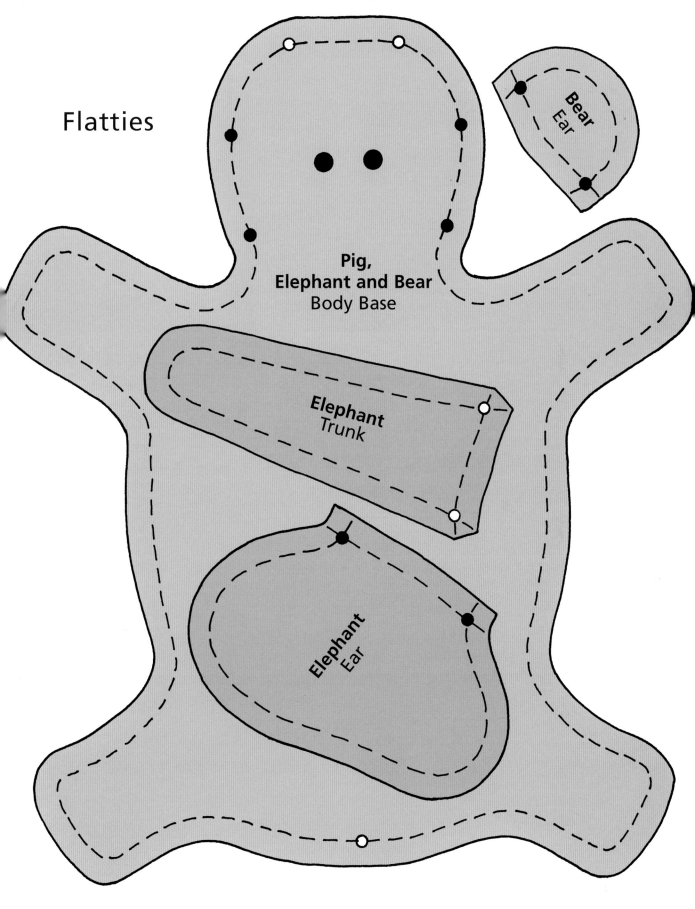

Flatties

Bear
Ear

Pig,
Elephant and Bear
Body Base

Elephant
Trunk

Elephant
Ear

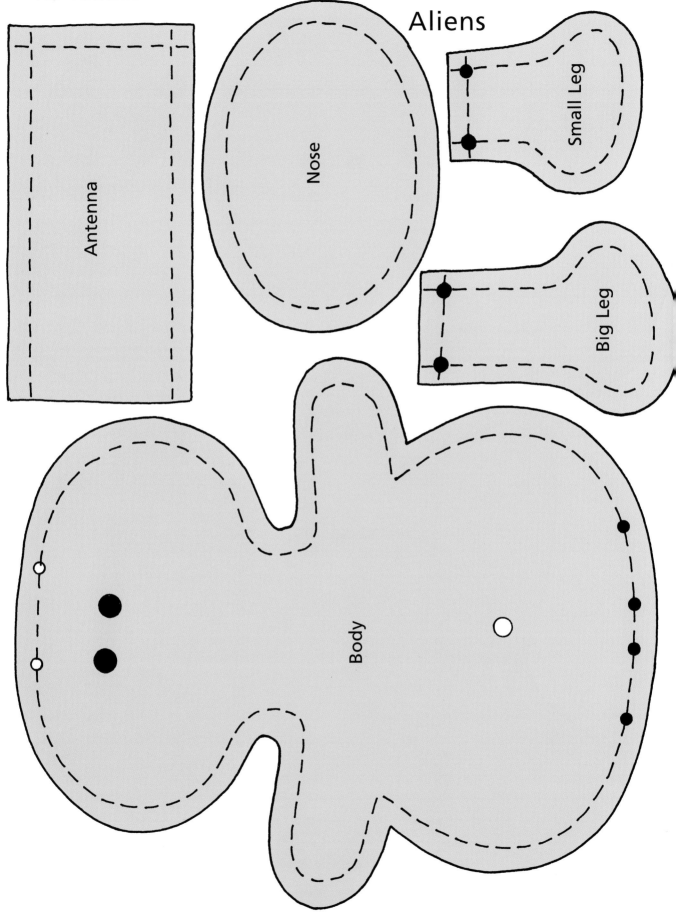

Antenna

Nose

Aliens

Small Leg

Big Leg

Body

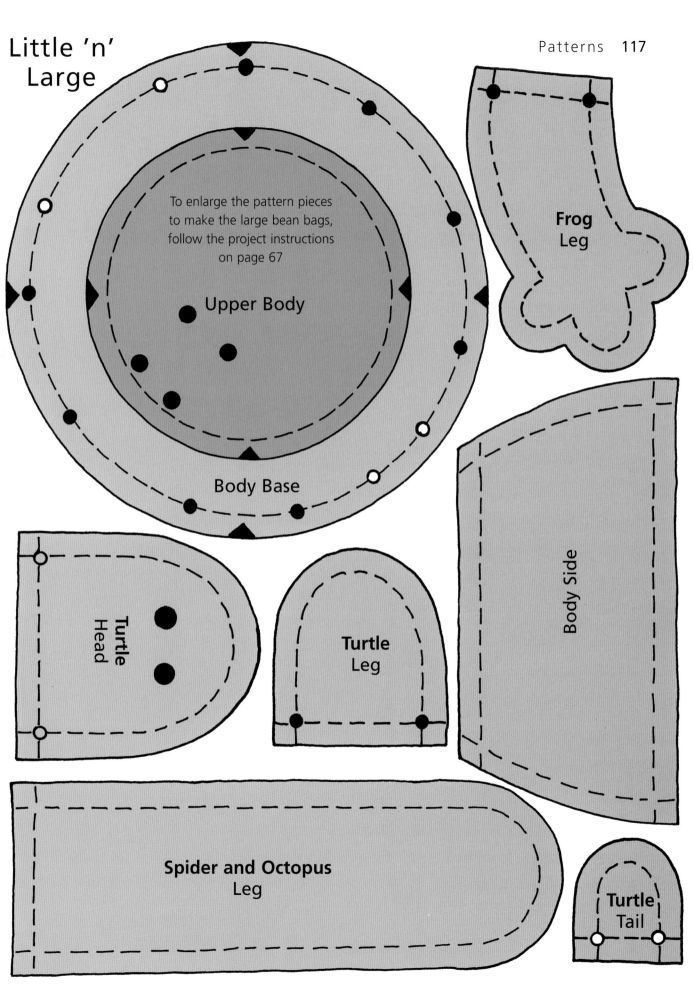

Little 'n' Large

To enlarge the pattern pieces to make the large bean bags, follow the project instructions on page 67

Upper Body

Body Base

Frog Leg

Body Side

Turtle Head

Turtle Leg

Spider and Octopus Leg

Turtle Tail

Knobbly Knees

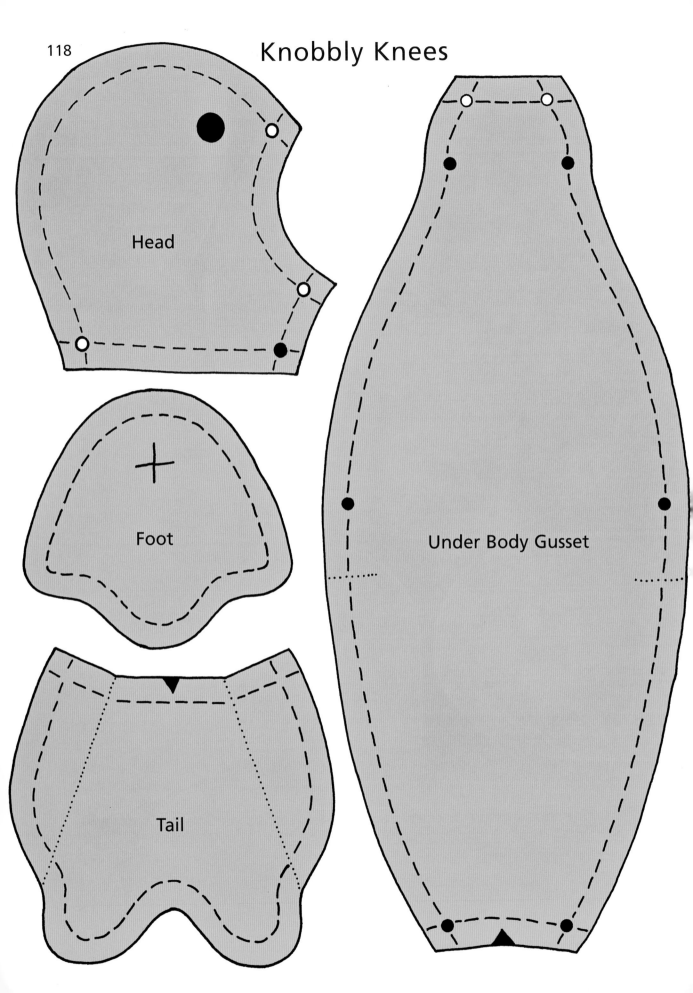

Head

Foot

Tail

Under Body Gusset

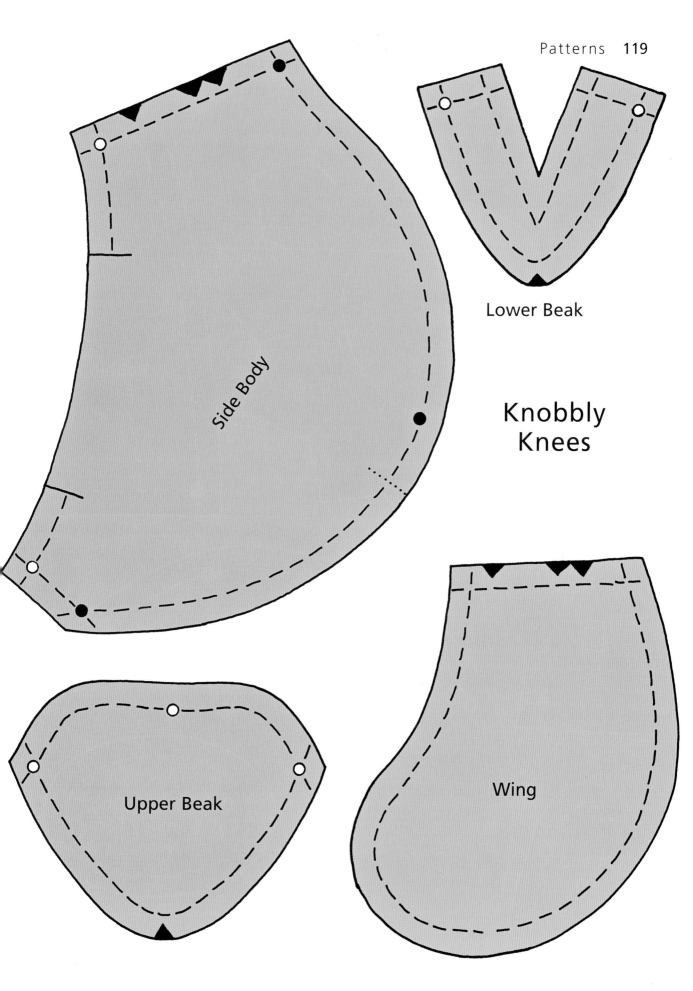

Lower Beak

Side Body

Knobbly
Knees

Upper Beak

Wing

Happy Heads

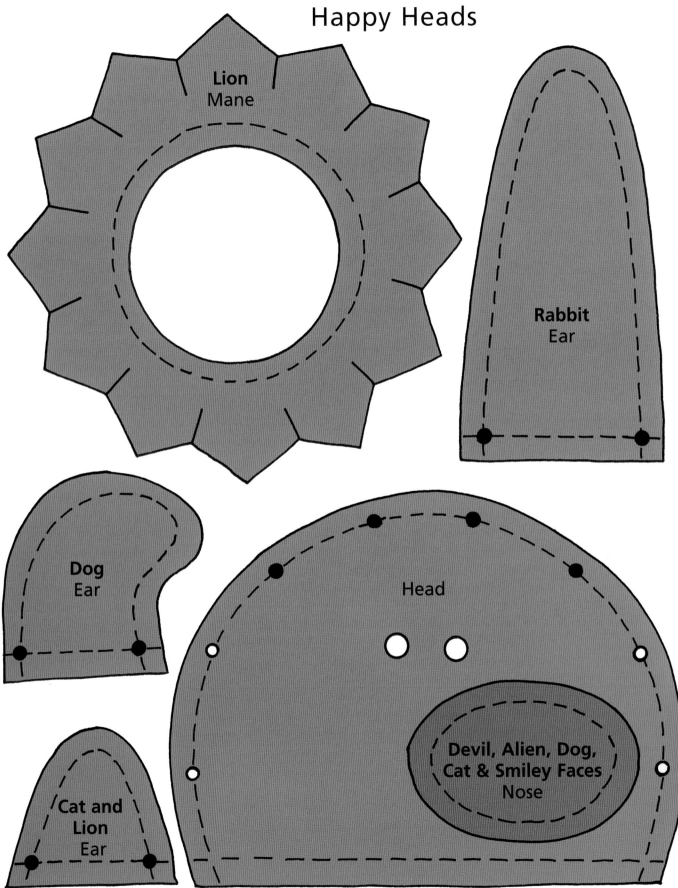

Lion
Mane

Rabbit
Ear

Dog
Ear

Head

**Devil, Alien, Dog,
Cat & Smiley Faces**
Nose

**Cat and
Lion**
Ear

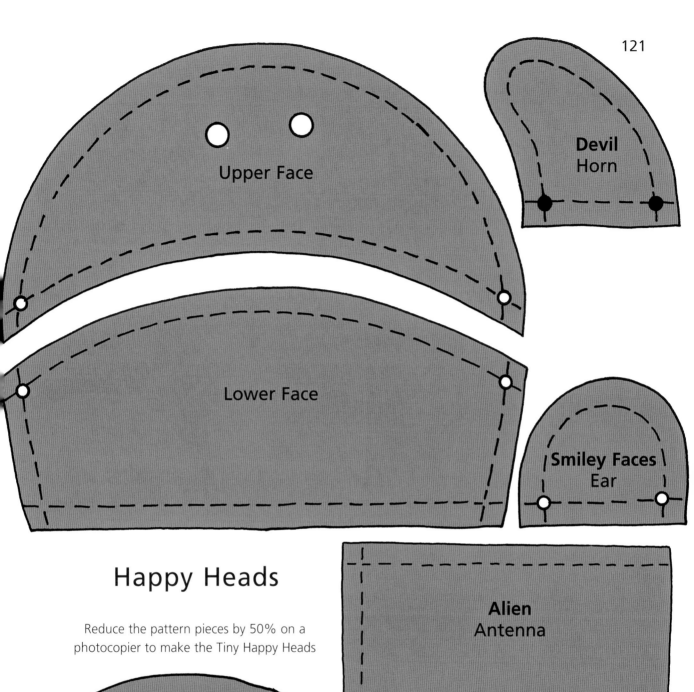

Upper Face

Devil
Horn

Lower Face

Smiley Faces
Ear

Alien
Antenna

Happy Heads

Reduce the pattern pieces by 50% on a
photocopier to make the Tiny Happy Heads

**Lion, Rabbit, Cat, Dog
and Smiley Faces**
Muzzle and Cheeks

Base

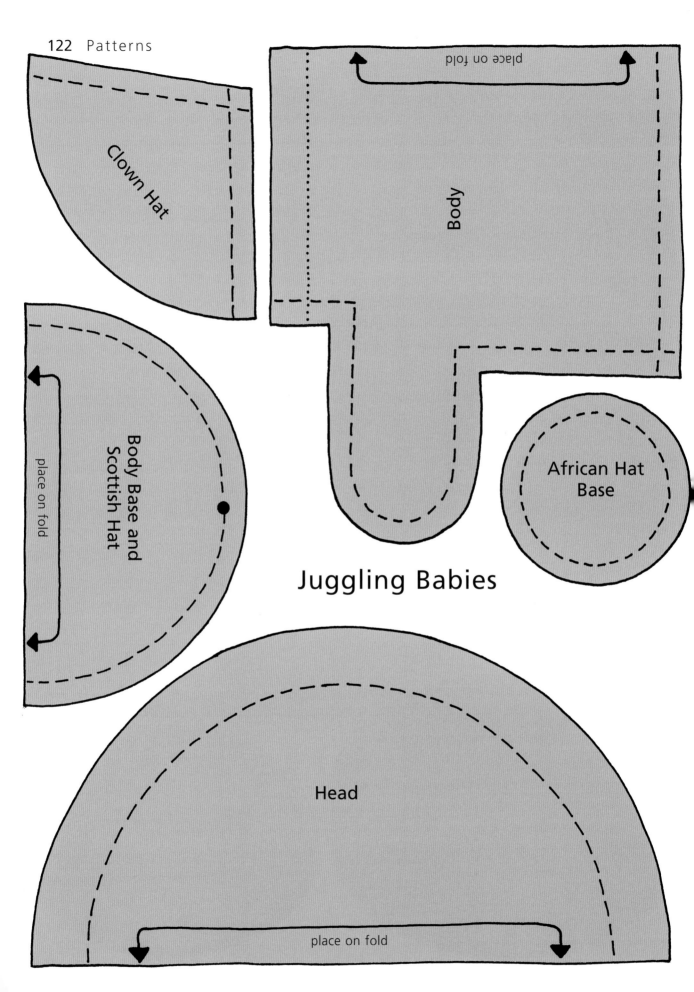

Clown Hat

place on fold

Body

Body Base and
Scottish Hat

place on fold

African Hat
Base

Juggling Babies

Head

place on fold

Hanging Around

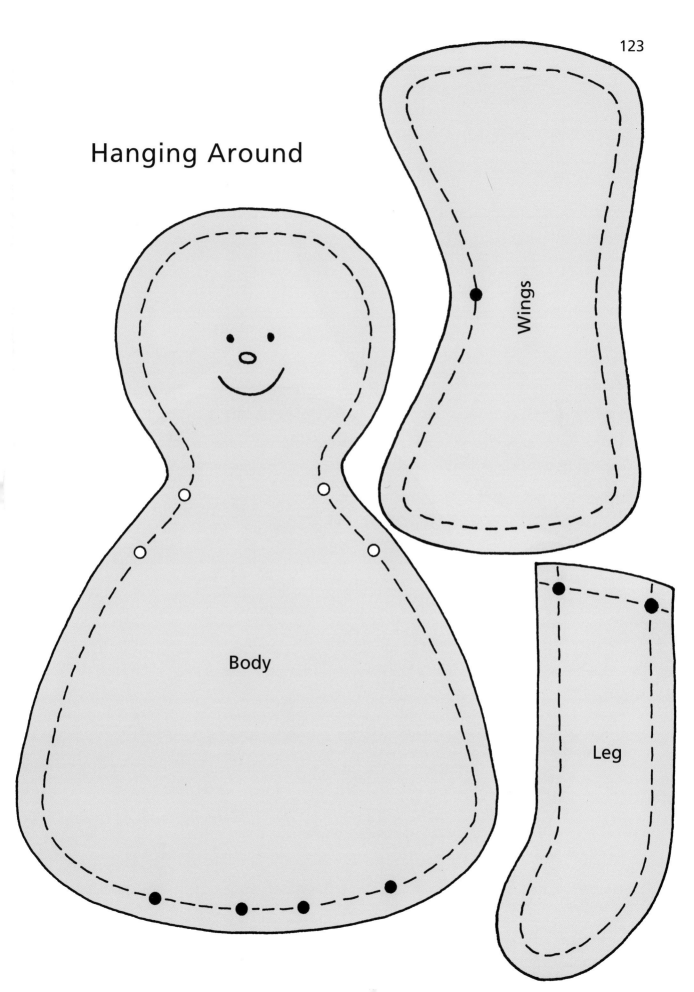

Wings

Body

Leg

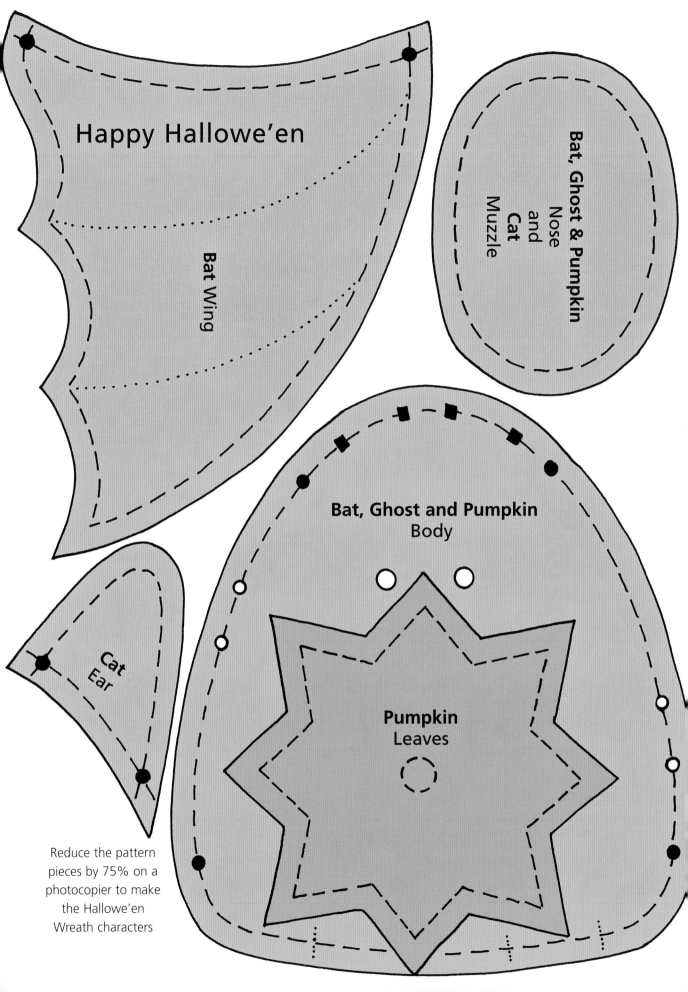

Happy Hallowe'en

Bat Wing

Bat, Ghost & Pumpkin
Nose
and
Cat
Muzzle

Bat, Ghost and Pumpkin
Body

Cat
Ear

Pumpkin
Leaves

Reduce the pattern
pieces by 75% on a
photocopier to make
the Hallowe'en
Wreath characters

Happy Hallowe'en

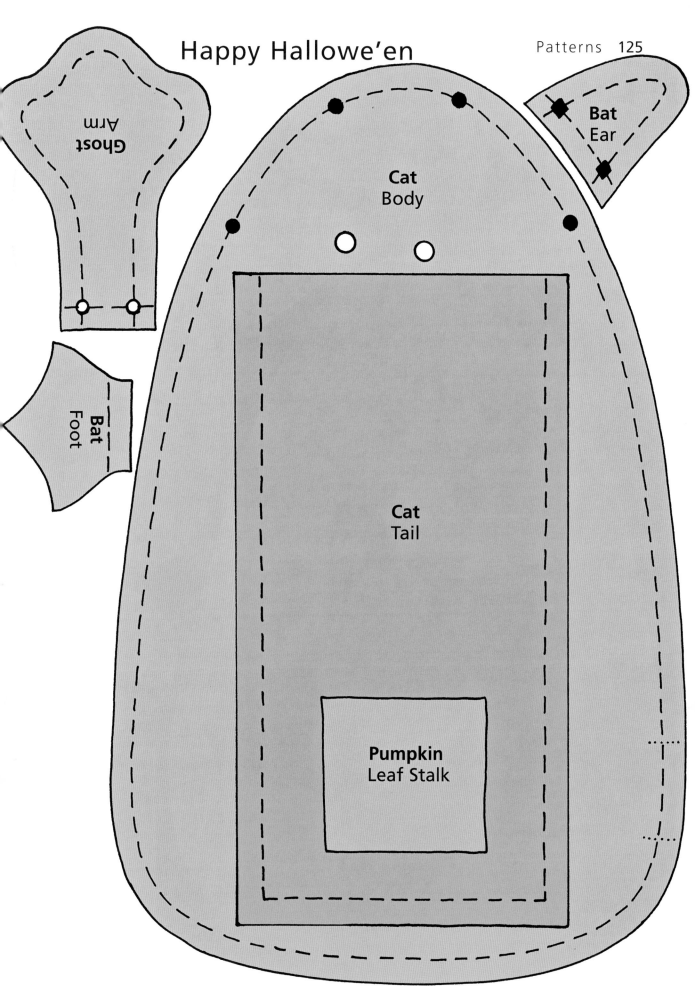

Ghost
Arm

Bat
Ear

Cat
Body

Bat
Foot

Cat
Tail

Pumpkin
Leaf Stalk

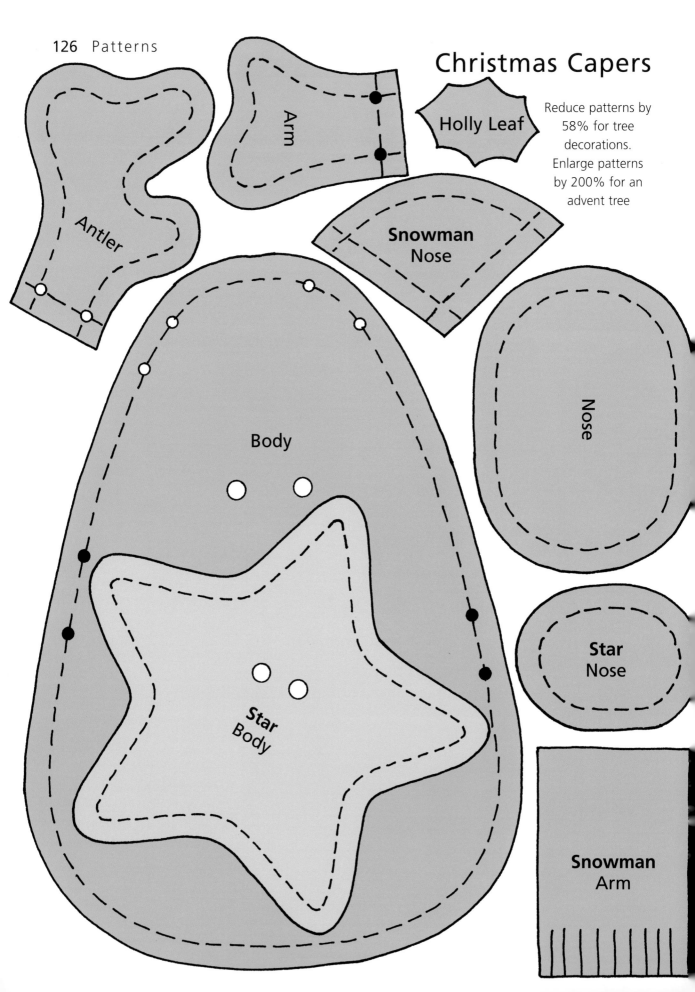

Christmas Capers

Reduce patterns by 58% for tree decorations. Enlarge patterns by 200% for an advent tree

Antler

Arm

Holly Leaf

Snowman Nose

Nose

Body

Star Nose

Star Body

Snowman Arm

STOCKISTS

If you want any further information about the products used in this book, catalogues, price lists or local stockists from any of the suppliers listed, contact them direct by post or phone. Please remember to always include a stamped self-addressed envelope. If you contact them by phone, they will be able to tell you if there is any charge for the catalogue or price list.

Rose & Hubble Ltd, 2–4 Relay Road, White City, London W12 7SJ.
Tel: 0181 749 8822 or Fax: 0181 740 9106 for the name of your nearest stockist.
All projects (except the Flat Face Friends Sheep Rug) used fleece and fur fabrics supplied by Rose & Hubble. These fabrics are available from fabric stores and haberdashery (notions) departments in major department stores.
.

Fred Aldous Ltd, P.O. Box 135, 37 Lever Street, Manchester M1 1LW.
Tel: 0161 236 2477. Fax: 0161 236 6075.
E-mail: Aldous@btinternet.com
Fred Aldous Ltd supplied the sheep fun fur, plastic beans, calico, fabric pens, pom-poms and safety noses and eyes (with the exception of the pink eyes for the flamingo and the brown eyes). You can purchase a large range of art and craft materials and equipment direct from their shop or by mail order.

ACKNOWLEDGEMENTS

This book was completed in double-quick time and I would like to give a big thank you to everyone who helped with and contributed to this book, especially: Cheryl Brown and Brenda Morrison at David & Charles, and to Doreen Montgomery, for their help with the production of this book. Thanks to Rose & Hubble and Fred Aldous for supplying the products and materials when I needed them urgently!

INDEX

Page numbers in **bold** refer to patterns; page numbers in *italics* refer to illustrations

Aliens, *56*, 57, 76, **116**, **120-1**
Allowances, seam, 12
Angel, 87, **123**
Antennae, 57, 76, **116**, **121**
Antlers, 97, **126**
Arms, 38, 42, 86, 91, 96, 98, **103**, **110**, **125**

Babies, 80-3, *80-1*, **122**
Balls, polysterene, 62, 67
Bat, 90, 93, **124-5**
Beak, 43, 68, 70, **111**, **119**
Beans, plastic, 6, 7, 9, 16
Bear, flat, 59, **114-15**; polar, *44*, 46-7, **100-1**; teddy, 20-2, **102-4**
Beaver, 28-9, **105-6**, **108-9**
Bell, 97
Bill, 30, **109**
Braid, 96, 98

Calico, 54, 67, 85-7
Cat, 77, 88, 89, 93, **120-1**, **124-5**
Cheeks, 14, 76, 89, **121**
Christmas tree, *94*, 96, **126**
Coat-hanger, 93
Cow, *34*, 35, 41-2, **110-12**
Crocodile, *26*, 31, **105-6**, **108-9**
Crow, *68*, 69-70, **118-19**
Cutting out, 11

Devil, 76-7, **120-1**
Dog, *19*, 25, 78, **102-4**, **120-1**
Doll, *84-5*, 86, **123**
Dragon, *27*, 32-3, **105-6**, **108-9**
Duck, 35, *35*, 43, **111-12**
Duck-billed platypus, 30, **106-9**

Ears, 21, 29, 32-3, 37, 42, 46, 49, 59, 61, 75, 89, **101-2**, **104-5**, **112-15**, **120-1**, **124-5**
Elastic, 60, 61, 65, 79, 86, 87, 89
Elephant, 61, **114-15**
Enlarging, 10, 54, 55, 67, 95, 126
Eyes, 7, 12, 16 and *passim*

Fabrics, 6, 7, 9, 11; pile, 11
Faces, 12-13, 37, 53-5 *passim*,
74-9, **108**, **111-13**, **120-1**
Feet, 12, 15, 43, 47, 69, 90, **101**, **106**, **112-13**, **118**, **125**
Felt, 90
Fillings, 6, 7, 9, 16
Fingers, 15, 98
Flamingo, *68*, 71, **118-19**
Fleece, 6, 9, 11, 53-5, 57, 64-6, 69, 71-3, 75-9, 91, 92
Fridge magnets, 74, 79
Frog, 64, 67, 78-9, **117**, **120-1**
Fur, fun, 53, 55

Ghost, 91, 93, **124-5**
Glue, 16, 93

Hair, 76, 82
Halo, 87
Hats, *80-1*, 83, 98, **122**
Hoof, 42, **110**, **111**
Horns, 42, 48, 77, **101**, **110**, **121**
Horse, 45, 49-50, **100-1**

Koala, 24, **102-4**

Leaves, 97, **124**, **126**
Legs, 57, 64-5, 69-73 *passim*, **102**, **105**, **110-11**, **116-17**, **123**
Leopard, *34*, 35, 36-9, **110-12**
Lining bag, 7, 16, *17*
Lion, 78, **120-1**
Lycra, 57, 90

Mane, 50, 51, 78, **120**
Monkey, *34*, 35, 40, **110-12**
Mouth, 12, 15, 39, 64, 66, 76, 77, 79, 91, 98
Muzzle, 12-14 *passim*, 39, 77, 89, **112**, **121**, **124**

Needles, 8
Nose, 7, 12-14 *passim*, 16, 29, 57, 60, 76, 77, 82, 90, 94, 98, **114**, **116**, **120**, **124**, **126**
Nostrils, 42, 60

Octopus, 65, 67, **117**

Parrot, 73, **118-19**
Patterns, 6, 10, 99-126
Paws, 38, **103**, **110**, **112**
Pens, marker, 9, 11, 86, 87
Pig, 60, **114-15**

Pillow, 52, *52*, 54
Pins, 8
Pom-poms, 23, 28, 29, 36, 39, 40, 57, 59, 77, 78, 83, 89, 96-8, *passim*
Pumpkin, 92, 93, **124-5**

Rabbit, *18*, 23, 77, **102-4**, **120-1**
Reducing, 10, 74, 79, 93, 126
Reindeer, 97, **126**
Rhino, *44*, 45, 48, **100-1**
Ribbon, 49-51 *passim*, 75, 86, 87, 93, 97
Rolled cylinders/tubes, 16, 69, 79, 92, 98
Rug, 52, *52*, 55

Safety, 7
Scarf, 98
Scissors, 8
Scrunchies, hair, 74, 79
Seagull, 72, **118-19**
Sequins, 87
Sheep, *52*, 53, **113**
Snowman, *94*, 97-8, **126**
Spider, 65, 67, **117**
Stars, 93, 98, **126**
Stitches, 12-13

Tag, 17
Tail, 22, 25, 29-31, 38-40 *passim*, 50, 51, 60, 72, 89, **101**, **103**, **109-10**, **112-14**, **117-18**
Tape, 49-51 *passim*
Thimble, 8
Threads, 9; embroidery, 9, 81
Toes, 12, 15, 38
Trunk, 61, **115**
Turtle, 66, 67, **117**
Twigs, 93

Velour, 9, 11 and *passim*

Wadding/batting 55, 93
Washers, 7, 16
Whiskers, 13, 15, 39, 77, 89
Wings, 33, 42, 69, 72, 73, 87, 89, **109**, **112**, **119**, **123-4**
Wool, 49-51 *passim*, 75, 76
Wreath, 93, **124-5**

Zebra, 45, *45*, 51, **100-1**
Zippers, 74, 79